She Solves Crimes Supernaturally . . .

Torn from the depths of her being, the visions appear to Dorothy Allison.

The mutilated body of a child . . .

The face of a nameless killer . . .

The hidden grave of a too-trusting teenager . . .

It began when Dorothy was fourteen. She "saw" white-ribboned lilies on the door, and knew her father would die that night.

Twenty-eight years later, early on a Sunday morning, Dorothy awoke from a painful dream. She had seen the body of a blond boy, floating.

Haunted by the child's image, she went to skeptical police.

And her controversial career as a psychic detective began . . .

DOROTHY ALLISON:
A Psychic Story

DOROTHY ALLISON
A PSYCHIC STORY

**DOROTHY ALLISON
AND SCOTT JACOBSON**

A JOVE BOOK

Requests for permission to make copies of any part
of the work should be mailed to: Permissions,
Jove Publications, Inc., 200 Madison Avenue,
New York, NY 10016

First Jove edition published September 1980

10 9 8 7 6 5 4 3 2 1

Printed in the United States of America

Jove books are published by Jove Publications, Inc.,
200 Madison Avenue, New York, NY 10016

Dorothy Allison and I wish to thank the following for their help and understanding: Maria O. Mirucki; Carmen A. Orechio, Director of Public Safety, Nutley, N. J.; Detective Sal Lubertazzi and Phyllis Lubertazzi; Deputy Chief Sal Dimichino; Detective Don Vicaro; Lieutenant Detective Richard Serafin; Detective Neil M. Forte; Chief Harold N. Gingrich, Sr.; State Trooper Paul D. Weachter; Chief Neil J. Behan; Detective Al Darden; Major Patricia Hanges; Lieutenant Gary C. Witt, Sr.; Fitz Ormon Clarke, Jr.; Larry Egan; Bob McDowell; Louis A. Giovanetti; J. Wallace LaPrade; Detective Sergeant George Homa; Detective Richard Rufino; and Investigator Gus Doyle.

We would also like to thank Dr. Richard Ribner; Bill and Ellen Jacobson; Lydia Kurscics; Ann Hazewski; Ruth Wyler; Nancy Locascio; John and Carol Hennessy; Joseph and Francis Carlucci; Jane and Richard Kline; Rosemary and Ralph Ferrara; Yolanda and Dr. Lawrence Giuffra; Bill Jenkins; Robert Cox and Ken Pfeiffer, authors of *Missing Person;* Beverly Lewis; Helen Kramer; Ronald F. Thomas; and Dan Farrell Davis.

S.J.

Author's Note

Psychic abilities such as Dorothy Allison's are an uncommon phenomenon. In this book I have not attempted to give a scientific explanation of psychic phenomena, but rather have related the stories of some of Dorothy Allison's most interesting cases.

Material for this book was gathered from several sources. Dorothy's own retelling of the stories has been supported by newspaper and magazine articles and signed affidavits from many of the parties involved. In most cases, the families of the victims have cooperated fully, regardless of the fact that the interviews stirred unpleasant memories. Many of the law-enforcement officers involved have also given generously of their time in recounting their experiences with the psychic detective. This book is a testimony to these people as well as to the marvelous work of Dorothy Allison.

In some instances, the names and facts surrounding certain characters in the cases have been changed to protect people's privacy. In such instances, any similarities to real people are purely coincidental and unintentional.

S.J.

Chapter 1

"How's your momma?" Mrs. Costa asked Dorothy as the girl's eyes bounced from pastry to pastry displayed in the glass case.

"She's okay," Dorothy replied, not letting her attention be diverted from the promise of a fresh pastry.

Mrs. Costa, a large Italian woman with silver-black hair wrapped firmly around her head, counted out rolls and placed them one by one into a white paper bag. She moved slowly under the oppressive heat of the July day. Not only was there little respite from the sun, but the baking ovens generated intense heat, and she had to blot her forehead and chin with a red cloth all day.

"Oh, *santa mia*," the robust woman exclaimed. "Did you hear all the noise yesterday? Too much for me," she said, running the cloth under her chin. "This is no way to celebrate such an important holiday. No good for my heart." She pounded her large breast with her fist.

"Did you see the wonderful rockets in the sky?" Dorothy's eyes lit up. "I love to see fireworks."

"Did you go by the water?" the woman inquired.

The girl nodded her head. "Taddo took us down. He says New York City has the best fireworks in the world."

The woman mumbled something in Italian about New York City being the devil across the way.

"Your poppa, is he better?" Mrs. Costa asked.

"I don't know. He only has a bad cough, but the doctor wanted to test him at the hospital."

Mrs. Costa rubbed her hand over the cabinets behind the counter. "These beautiful cabinets and counters were made by your father's hands. He is a good man." She turned to Dorothy. "Your poor momma is cooking for all those children and going to the hospital in this heat. *Carissimo*! I do not know how she does it. God must be close to her."

Mrs. Costa wagged a finger at Dorothy. "You better run home with this bread so she doesn't worry."

Dorothy stretched her short arms over the counter top and received the large bag.

"Wait," Mrs. Costa said. "I'll be right back." She lumbered into the back area and disappeared. Dorothy stood before the glass counter and gazed at her reflection. At fourteen Dorothy was as high as the rim of the counter. Her brown hair fell below her shoulders. Her large, llamalike eyes had soft brown rings around them, giving her strong brow a gentle prominence and her complexion a deep richness.

She looked into the glass and stared into her eyes. Something was strange. As she looked through the glass at the displayed breads, images began to appear that caused her to rub her eyes, thinking her vision was blurred.

The face of a man appeared, suspended in air. The images of the bread, her reflection, and the face moved one over the other. The girl stood transfixed for a moment, gliding between worlds of consciousness, her eyes staring directly into their own reflection. Dorothy saw the outlines of the man's face. She could not make out the features, but the face moved back and forth, teasing her line of focus.

"Here you go," Mrs. Costa's voice sang out. "Here's a fresh cannoli for you." The woman walked around the counter and handed Dorothy the pastry wrapped in waxed paper.

"You help your poor momma and tell her I'm praying

12

for your poppa." She pinched the girl's cheek so hard it smarted.

Dorothy walked out of the bakery and stood on the glaring sidewalk. The streets of Jersey City were hot and dusty on July 5, 1939. The sun baked the streets that sprawled endlessly from the Hudson River through the neighborhoods that rolled out under the shadow of burgeoning New York City. Nibbling her pastry, Dorothy walked down Westside Avenue, the main thoroughfare linking Jersey City to Bayonne, Hoboken, and other Hudson River towns. She walked, however, without seeing the world. Something was happening that she could not explain. The reflection in the bakery shop haunted her.

Under the shadowed network of branches, Dorothy approached her home slowly. Her family lived in the upper floor of a two-story gray shingled house. Dorothy shared a bedroom with four sisters, while five brothers slept in the next room. Dorothy's oldest sister, Mary, had recently entered a convent. Dorothy had been pleased when she left, because she disliked her sister's fanatacism. Mary reminded her too much of the nuns at Dorothy's school, Our Lady of Victory, who often beat her for her disobedience.

Dorothy sat on the steps of her home, wondering what she was experiencing. It was not uncommon for her to see something in her dreams that she had never seen in real life. Countless hours had been spent in half-consciousness, staring at the ceiling as an endless parade of humanity passed in review. Dorothy passively watched the parade, wondering what significance the dreams might have. Her soft eyes were powerless to control the visions; they came and went without provocation, and only when she relaxed into sleep.

From the steps Dorothy watched a train of ants cross the gnarled oak roots that made up the little yard, and suddenly her vision blurred. In the graying shadow of the afternoon the lines of the man's face reappeared. The vague outlines of a jaw came together over the roots and earth.

She rubbed her eyes: in the dark behind her closed eyelids, the face became clearer. She opened her eyes, the ants

13

once again in focus, the lines of the face as real as the hundreds of creatures marching in the dirt. A long narrow jawline, and two long, drooping ears fleshed out before her.

The gossamer-like apparition disappeared quickly. She turned around to see if her mother or sisters were watching from above. No one else had seen what she had witnessed. Is it real? she asked herself.

Looking at the screen door, Dorothy began to see a new image, this time much clearer and more detailed. Crisp, white flowers adorned the door. They were long white lilies dressed in green leaves.

"Hi, Dot," the voice of a girl called out from down the block.

Dorothy turned from her vision and looked down the sidewalk. Her friend Vicky waved at her from two houses away.

"Hiya, Vicky," Dorothy said to her, coming out of the trance.

Vicky, one of Dorothy's schoolmates at Our Lady of Victory, stood before her on the stoop, her thin legs dropping like matchsticks out of her plaid skirt.

"Where's your brother?" Dorothy asked the dark-haired girl.

"Why do you want my brother?" Vicky squealed. A smile spread across her face as she considered the prospects. "I know why you want my brother. You think he's in love with you."

Dorothy reddened. "No, I don't, you idiot. He owes me a dime and I want it now." She stamped her foot in front of Vicky's feet.

"How come he owes you money?" Vicky inquired.

"I bet him I could beat him out of church and I did, by a hundred miles," she announced proudly. Escaping from church was Dorothy's favorite sport.

"Can you come bowling with us tomorrow night?" Vicky asked.

"I don't know," Dorothy replied, her mood changing quickly. She looked at her friend and then, as if instinctively, she turned around and looked again at the front door.

"I can't go bowling tomorrow night," she said, turning

14

back to Vicky. This time her voice was serious. She pointed to the door, where she saw the white crepe affixed, and two velvet ribbons dangling to the ground. "There's a white crepe on the door," Dorothy said, her voice sounding hollow, insubstantial.

"What crepe on the door, Dot? What are you talking about?" Vicky shrugged her shoulders.

Dorothy looked at the earth: the outline of the man's face again floated defiantly, clearer than before, but not clear enough for her to recognize the face.

The mental alchemy of images and thoughts tossing in her mind began to coalesce. Dorothy was beginning to understand. White flowers. Lilies. She thought of Easter, Christ, death.

Without further consideration, she turned to Vicky and said, "My father will be dead tomorrow night, and I won't be able to go bowling. That's why there's white crepe on the door."

"There's nothing on the door, Dot," Vicky insisted.

"He has a bad cough and they're checking it out," she said to her friend. "No one said he's going to die. I just see it. I saw it at the bakery in the glass. Mrs. Costa didn't see it, either." She stopped short, realizing the import of her words.

The screen door opened and Appolonia, Dorothy's mother, stood behind her. A strong woman of medium height, Appolonia moved with an air of certainty and purpose, her maternal instincts always alert.

"Dorothy," her mother said. "I've got to go to the hospital. Give me the bread and finish your other chores."

"I've got to go now, anyway," Vicky said uncomfortably. "See you at the park, Dot, unless you change your mind about bowling."

Appolonia took the bakery bag but did not go back into the house. Dorothy, still sitting on the steps, looked down. She was aware of her mother's presence behind her, lingering as if in afterthought. For a moment the two were in a silent orbit all their own. Dorothy sat with her fear and stared at the tree roots. Appolonia sighed and closed the door behind her as she made her way up the stairs.

Dorothy relaxed when she knew her mother was gone.

15

She wanted to tell her about her vision, but she feared the repercussions of revealing such horrors. More than anything else, she did not want to hurt her mother.

The crisp, white chalkiness of the lilies glowed before her as if she could hold out her hand and feel their soft textures. The lilies of death, as her mother called them, had an eerie beauty that held Dorothy's round gaze. Death, not her own, would influence her life greatly. One day Dorothy would wake up and see death at work, but many dreams and years would pass before that night.

At this moment all Dorothy wanted was to be held by her mother and told that nothing unusual was happening. Fear kept her silent, however. Fear of having told Vicky of her father's death; of having accepted the lilies as real; of having seen the face in the bakery reflection; of not dreaming, but *seeing*.

That night Dorothy lay awake in the darkness of her room, her sisters sleeping around her. She felt confused. The dark, vague image of her father's face on a pillow, still and unnatural, haunted her. Then the white crepe appeared, two velvet streamers flowing down the door, swinging in the air in eerie silence. The door opened and closed silently as the feet of mourners passed quickly in quiet sadness.

As never before, Dorothy was aware of her prescience physically and emotionally. Previously, she had discounted entire dream sequences as meaningless. Now, for the first time in her life, she knew what she saw was true; she doubted nothing. The grim pallor of her father's face was as her mother last saw him. Dorothy would have to wait for time to pass for corroboration. She was alone with her vision.

Softly Dorothy slipped out of her room, moving in the darkness toward her mother's room, where candlelight still glowed into the hallway through the open doorway. She stood in the doorway of her parents' bedroom. Her mother had not yet returned from the hospital.

In half-waking, half-sleeping trance Dorothy stared at the table next to her mother's dresser. On a shiny red cloth stood two rows of statues: ceramic figures, silent and ceremonious. In the candlelight the ceramic figures radiated a pasty, unnatural color.

Dorothy thought of her father, his white smile always hiding behind his soft, faded moustache. She looked at the beautiful tall oak armoire that stood in the corner of the bedroom. Her father had lovingly crafted it for Appolonia, and Dorothy recalled how her mother cried each time she showed it to a friend.

Tears came to her own eyes as she thought of her father cooking the Sunday pasta. He always called it "Appolonia's Day of Rest" meal. His daughters delighted in spending the afternoon helping Poppa in the kitchen and then serving their parents with loving formality.

Dorothy could hear the voices of her mother's friends chanting Latin liturgy, as they did in the afternoon. She saw Appolonia holding her beads and intoning prayers before her table of statues. The women knelt on the worn bedroom carpet, allowing Appolonia to lead them. They came not only to pray, but to listen, as well, to the woman who could see the future—the woman in whom God had vested a special light; whose soft tongue spoke of future tragedies and hazards, of blessings and joys. They also came to her in the nighttime, when she huddled in her kitchen, praying for her family and friends, advising them.

Only God could have given her the ability to see into the future. "It is a test of will and belief in God," she had told her friends.

"It is a gift with a sting," she had said to her daughter.

Dorothy looked again at the religious figures. They made her feel uncomfortable. She looked at the clock beside the statues. It was 12:50.

Dorothy went to the living room and crouched in a corner of the old sofa. There she sat in the stillness of the night, vigilant in a household of sleeping children. She floated between waking and sleeping, holding herself for comfort.

After awhile she heard steps coming up the walk. She knew it was her mother. She also knew what her mother was going to tell her. Tears came to the girl's eyes.

Appolonia entered the room moments later, moving slowly, lugubriously. The two figures, mother and daughter, embraced in the darkness, sharing the grief of the father's death. But Appolonia felt more than sadness in the embrace; holding her daughter, she wept tears of fear, as well. Appolonia's dread that one of her children might share her visionary power was founded, she now realized, in fact. She needed no more evidence.

"He is with God now," Appolonia whispered. "We will have much work to do, but God will help us, I know."

The young girl responded to her mother's words with another warm embrace. Her mother looked around the quiet room, as if envisioning what would follow in the next few days.

"I must have extra candles," she said, beginning a mental list. She turned to the front door.

"Tomorrow a white crepe will tell the world of our sadness. Good night, my child." She kissed Dorothy's forehead and looked into her eyes. "Do not be frightened of the world you see. You must believe in God's wisdom." She turned and walked slowly to her room.

Dorothy sat in the darkness, picturing the crepe her mother spoke of and trying to understand her feelings and thoughts. She had never believed in God as her mother and her sisters did, so she doubted whether God would be of much help to her. She did believe, however, that difficult times were ahead. She was frightened.

Chapter 2

Their father's death was hard on all the family. Appolonia, crying and praying more often, seemed to lose some of herself. She soon made the decision to take the vows of the Third Order, vows of a widow similar to those taken by nuns, devoting her time and energies almost exclusively to the church.

To help Appolonia with the work and the management of the children's lives, Mary, Dorothy's oldest sister, returned from the convent. Dorothy wasn't pleased to see her. Mary would correct Dorothy at dinner and insist she do everything as God intended. Dorothy believed in God, and retained that faith all her life, but she didn't always like the way He delivered His messages. Nor did Dorothy receive any sympathy at home when she complained about her teacher, Sister Catherine, who sometimes meted out harsh punishments. Dorothy figured her sister, like a fellow union worker, would always be on the teacher's side.

Graduation from grammar school was an important day in Dorothy's life. Not only was she leaving Our Lady of Victory, a school that had imprisoned her restless nature, but on that same afternoon she had an adventure with three girl friends that she would remember all her life.

Without telling anyone, the girls went to Chinatown in New York City. They still wore the white blouses and white skirts in which they had graduated. Arm in arm they walked nervously along congested and noisy Canal Street. Barechested men shouted from windows above the street. The girls were intimidated at seeing all the huge trucks and the factories found in this neighborhood.

They didn't know exactly where they were heading, but they were hungry and wanted to try eating in a Chinese restaurant. But even more important, they wanted to have their fortunes told.

The girls passed several restaurants before stopping at one. A smiling, round-faced man standing behind the window saw them trying to read the menu and waved them down the steps. He was kind and helped them order, though they never knew what they ate.

Maria, one of Dorothy's friends, asked the Chinese man if he knew of any fortune-tellers. He smiled a row of bad teeth and pointed down the street. "Mrs. Wong," he said, "she sees everything."

Mrs. Wong's small fortune-teller's sign stood in the window on a piece of faded green silk next to a rosary and a cross. The girls slowly walked into the dark room, and before their eyes adjusted, they heard the cheerful chirp of the fortune-teller. She was bright-eyed and small, the same height as the girls. She shook hands with each of them and bowed. Mrs. Wong led them through curtains into another room where they sat around a dimly lit table covered with green silk, like that in the window but less faded.

The girls were scared, giggling and holding onto one another as though on a spook ride. Mrs. Wong gazed at each of them, never saying a thing but looking into their eyes.

Without warning she reached for Dorothy's hand and held it out for everyone to see. All eyes were on Dorothy's palm as Mrs. Wong ran a long fingernail over the tiny channels. No one said a word; no one giggled.

Mrs. Wong first said that Dorothy would have a long life. At fourteen that didn't mean too much to the girl. The fortune-teller then talked about problems she would have with members of her family and said that later in life she would stand alone. Dorothy had no idea what that could mean, so she wasn't disturbed.

Then Mrs. Wong said that Dorothy would be married within two years. Maria, Rose, and Katherine all lunged forward as if they had received an electric shock. Everyone looked into Dorothy's hand for a glimpse of the man she would marry. As if that wasn't enough, the seer said that she would have a child within three years!

Dorothy felt as though her heart had stopped. Married at sixteen, she thought to herself. That frightened her. Her father was dead, her mother grieving, and now she was to be shipped off with a husband. She felt lonely and abandoned. Having a child was not nearly as frightening as getting married: she had no idea where children came from.

Dorothy wondered how Mrs. Wong had known. The man Dorothy was to marry a year and a half later lived across the street from her. He was a tough little Irishman named Richard McSorley. What the two lacked in height—neither stretched over five feet—they made up for in temperament.

Two weeks after they met, Richard proposed marriage and Dorothy agreed, seeing the idea as an escape from the strictures of her own house, where the atmosphere had changed so much since her father's death. The young couple drove to Maryland for the marriage license, the longest trip Dorothy had ever taken. On the ride down she told Richard about Mrs. Wong's prediction coming true.

"A fortune-teller!" he exclaimed. "You went to a fortune-teller? I suppose you believe in spooks, too?"

His words hurt her. After that she was afraid to mention anything about the things she was seeing and in which she believed.

Sixteen and married, seventeen and pregnant, and at eighteen, a mother of a strong boy. Suddenly she was an adult. Before she knew it, her entire life had changed, and so did the way people treated her. Even though she had only moved across the street and down the block, the world was a very different place for her. Her mother still ran a tight ship in her home, but Dorothy was no longer part of it. And by now she had realized that God came first in her mother's eyes; all her visionary powers were devoted to Him.

During all the changes in Dorothy's life, she continued to have visions of her own. The fear and loneliness of her first vision had left her apprehensive and confused. Still too young to comprehend what had occurred, she took solace in the fact that Appolonia, too, saw things that others never saw.

At eighteen Dorothy had not yet learned that she could control what she was seeing. Sometimes, sitting with a friend or neighbor on the front stoop, she would say things that surprised people. She was talking from an inner vision, which they couldn't share.

One of Dorothy's closest bonds at the time was with her next-door neighbor, Nelly, a dark-haired Albanian woman who lived upstairs in the gray and white wooden house with her husband and three daughters. Her sister, Dodo, lived downstairs with her husband and two children. The two sisters had a habit of hanging out their windows and shouting messages to one another, impervious to the fact that all the neighbors could hear. It was during such an exchange that Dorothy had met them.

One day Dorothy and Nelly were sitting on the steps breaking pea pods and tossing the little peas into a huge silver soup pot. Nelly was much older than Dorothy and served not only as a friend, but as a motherly adviser as well. Nelly would often talk to Dorothy about raising children, offering her own special brand of wisdom.

On that day Nelly was worrying about the future of her daughter, Jeannine, who had a new boyfriend. She wondered if Jeannine would marry a rich husband and have lots of children.

When Dorothy told her that her daughter would marry not once, but twice, would have two children, and would be comfortable but never rich, Nelly looked at her in amazement.

"She will marry twice?" the stunned mother repeated.

"Twice," Dorothy nodded, watching the peas bounce into the pot.

"How can this be?" Nelly wondered. "No daughter of

mine can marry twice. It is not allowed." Nelly's voice was getting louder. "She will have to be happy with one husband, and I will tell her so."

"What if her first husband dies?" Dorothy interjected. "Couldn't she marry twice, then?" Dorothy had suddenly received a mental picture that convinced her Jeannine's first husband would leave her a widow.

"Oh, thank God," the mother exclaimed. "The family will be relieved to know she won't divorce."

Despite Nelly's relief, Dorothy could sense she was trying to figure out how her friend could know all about her daughter's future.

After a few minutes Nelly began again. "Dorothy, did you know that Mr. DeVito is sick? They put him in the hospital yesterday."

"No, I didn't know that," she said.

"Last week you told me he was going to be very sick. Remember? And I said you were crazy and better watch your tongue? How did you know he was going to be sick?" Nelly was hard in pursuit.

"I didn't," Dorothy said honestly. "When I was buying fruit last week, I saw him talking to Mrs. Menuchi. Suddenly I saw him in a hospital bed. That's all I know."

Nelly gave her a long, hard look. She didn't say a thing, but kept looking into Dorothy's eyes as if trying to see what her friend was seeing.

"You saw him in a hospital bed, just like that?" Nelly cocked her head to one side and rested it on her hand. "No one asked you if he was going to be sick?"

"No one asked me anything," Dorothy told her.

"Have you ever seen me in bed like that?" Nelly demanded.

Dorothy told her she had never seen her like that, and Nelly crossed herself and thanked God for her good health.

It wasn't easy for Dorothy to accept people's reactions to her, especially when they had already been told by neighbors or relatives that she had certain abilities. Nelly and Dodo spread the word about her throughout the neighborhood, not without adding embellishments of their own. Many of the neighbors knew that Appolonia had special visionary talents and felt that Dorothy had been chosen by God to follow in her footsteps.

Dorothy's extraordinary powers sometimes got the young woman into uncomfortable situations. One sunny spring day Dorothy was walking down the avenue, pushing her son in his stroller. In the distance she saw Father deSoto standing under a huge elm on the street. The tall, gaunt, young priest seemed to be resting.

Dorothy, not really wanting to talk to the man, slowed down and edged closer into the shadows of the high hedges. Suddenly her foot sank into a hole and Sam's stroller overturned, making enough noise to alarm the priest, who came over to help her.

Bending over the dark-haired tot, Father deSoto poked a finger at him. The child, already startled by the jolt to his stroller, bit the father's finger with unusual force.

Dorothy was embarrassed but once the stroller was righted and the child soothed, she and the priest continued to walk along the busy avenue. Uncomfortable with the silence, Dorothy decided to tell the priest about one of her recent dreams.

In her weekly confessionals Dorothy never spoke of the things she saw in her visions. She had long ago decided that the church knew enough about her from her mother and sisters. But today she decided to break her silence by telling the priest about a seemingly ordinary dream.

"This isn't part of confession or anything," Dorothy started, "but I had this dream the other night that you were in." Dorothy figured priests were included in the dreams of many young girls, so she assumed there was nothing unusual about her dream.

"We were all in church and you were just finishing the service when I saw a great big number on top of your head—the number eight. It just sort of floated there, and so did other numbers, while you talked about the church social and bingo night, which is tomorrow."

The priest walked along silently for a moment, hands clasped behind him, trying to figure out what Dorothy's dream meant. Though he was in his thirties, Father deSoto looked old. He was thin and wore gold-rimmed glasses.

Dorothy thought he was too serious-minded. The man was no fool, though. He knew that Appolonia was gifted with vision, which he believed gave her a special place with God. But Appolonia had never reported numbers appearing while bingo was being announced.

"Are you coming tomorrow night?" Father deSoto asked.

"Sure," Dorothy told him. "Richard and I wouldn't miss it for the world."

He stopped and looked at her for a second. "Keep it in mind, this dream you have had. Maybe God has given you a hint." He turned and walked in the opposite direction.

The following Sunday, Father deSoto made his way over to Dorothy after the service. He had been at the social and had watched the bingo winnings with interest.

"God has given you a special message," he said.

Dorothy knew he was aware of her winnings, so she could not fool him. She was sure one of her sisters would report them, if she didn't.

"Yes, sir. Number eight did all right for me." She took a deep breath. "I would like to share my winnings with the church, Father," Dorothy said unhappily.

"God will be very pleased with that," he said. "And anytime He gives you such messages, you may share them with me. I will help you with them."

Help, indeed! Dorothy thought to herself. She had learned a valuable lesson from the priest: money was to be made and kept in silence.

Appolonia was getting old, and her energy seemed to slacken daily. Everyone in the quiet, tree-lined neighborhood loved her. Her greatest joy was being with her grandchildren, for whom she always kept plenty of hard candy.

One day when Dorothy visited Appolonia, she found her in bed. Her mother looked tired. In fact she was only holding her life together through the strength of her beliefs and her trust in people. In two weeks the flame of life would go out, and Appolonia knew it.

"I see the face of God and I am ready," she said to Dorothy who sat quietly beside the bed. Appolonia reached out and took her daughter's hand.

"You are strong, my daughter. You are blessed by God with special gifts. For years I have watched and listened." She paused for a moment, holding Dorothy's gaze. Their eyes were the same deep brown, revealing their Mediterranean ancestry.

"Beware of your tongue," she warned sternly. "You will say things to people that they won't want to hear. Do not speak twice. If someone does not believe you the first time, do not say it again."

Dorothy nodded her head as if she were in church. She knew her mother would die soon. She looked around the candlelit room which was full of her mother's life—her few possessions that tied her to Italy, to God, and to her family. She looked at the old photograph of her parents, showing a sturdy, proud, young couple; at the saints' statues and Bible; the yellowed lace curtains; and the ceramic animals on the dresser.

These things, Dorothy thought, have only one owner, and she will soon be gone.

"You will marry twice in your lifetime," Appolonia declared. "You will have several children. You will be comfortable, I know. You will stand alone." Her voice was timeless as she unconsciously echoed the predictions Dorothy had heard years earlier, in Chinatown.

"My prayers have brought me special sight, and you too have it. Use it," she said with tears gently falling down her cheek, "as God would want. He gave it to you, and He alone can take it away."

When Appolonia died two weeks later, the white crepe on the door again was a reminder to Dorothy of her father's death, her own vision, and all the things her mother had said to her. She never doubted what Appolonia had told her. Appolonia had believed in herself, and Dorothy felt deeply that self-belief was her most important strength.

Oftentimes Dorothy wished she hadn't seen things, or hadn't reacted to visions before thinking what effect her words might have. Without being able to clearly recognize what was occurring, she would fall prey to sadness.

Once, several years after Appolonia's death, Nelly and Dorothy attended the funeral of their friend Serrita's father. After the service at the cemetery several mourners stood around with Serrita and her two sisters, reminiscing about the time when their father had paraded them around on his broad shoulders when they were youngsters. Nelly and Dorothy walked the sisters back toward their house, Dorothy saying farewell to them when they arrived at her corner.

Later that evening Dorothy went to Serrita's with freshly baked cakes in hand. As she approached the front steps, a picture of Serrita's husband, Jack, flashed before her. He had a devilish smile on his face. She didn't think much about it, though, and instead concentrated on the sadness of the occasion.

Serrita came to the door and the two women embraced. Serrita seemed glad to see Dorothy, but very disturbed. With tears in her eyes, she took Dorothy's arm and led her out onto the porch.

"Dorothy," she whispered, "I don't know how to tell you. Something terrible has happened and I don't want everyone to know."

"What is it, Serrita?" Dorothy asked.

The attractive woman looked around to be sure no one was listening. Dorothy knew that Jack had told his wife not to solicit advice from her. Many husbands disliked the things Dorothy told their wives, and warned them against her. Dorothy was hurt, but before she spoke, the same teasing image of Serrita's husband came to her again.

"During the funeral, while my poor father was being buried, we were robbed," Serrita said. "My mother's jewelry was stolen." She cried into her hands. "The money I had saved . . . it's gone, too. All of it. Oh God, it's too much for me."

Dorothy held Serrita in her arms while she cried. She knew instantly who was responsible for the theft, but she couldn't say anything to the weeping woman. Dorothy was frightened.

"Put this out of your mind for right now," Dorothy advised her. "We'll talk about it later. You have too much on your mind already."

She agreed to drop the matter for the time being, but she felt Dorothy knew something about it. Dorothy pleaded ignorance but said she would give some thought to the incident in the following days.

Two weeks later Dorothy was sitting on her front steps watching Sam feed pigeons, when Serrita walked up the sidewalk. Dorothy saw that she looked upset, so she sent Sam to Nelly's for more bread crumbs.

As soon as Sam walked away, Serrita began. "I think you know who stole my mother's jewelry."

Dorothy looked her in the eye. "Do you really want to know?"

"Yes," she demanded.

"Jack. Your husband stole the money and jewelry."

Serrita was shocked. She held her breath for a long time. The color of her complexion changed and tears rushed to her eyes.

"You're lying, Dorothy. It's not true," she screamed.

"If you don't want to believe me, then don't," Dorothy said defensively, holding back the sadness and confusion she was feeling. She felt grieved at her friend's reaction. "It's your choice," Dorothy told her.

Serrita got up and walked away without looking back at Dorothy. Dorothy watched her walk under the trees and fade away in the shadows, and her own heart was sinking. But Dorothy never said a word to anyone about what had occurred. Though everyone knew about the robbery, no one knew who did it.

Serrita didn't talk to Dorothy for two years. Then one day she suddenly appeared on Dorothy's doorstep. "Dorothy, can I talk to you for a minute?" she asked.

"Sure, sweetheart. Come on in. You look wonderful." Dorothy took her hand and led her into the kitchen. She could see Serrita was uncomfortable. Tears filled Serrita's eyes as she began to speak.

"I have something very hard to say," she told Dorothy.

Dorothy held her breath, knowing what the words would be.

"You were right about the robbery. Jack did steal the jewelry. For two years I've never said a word to anyone. Two awful years, and now I know it's true." She stopped to catch her breath. "Last night we had a fight and I told the bastard I knew he stole the ring and money. The truth was

28

in his face. He couldn't believe I knew. He said nothing to me about it. He just left the house, and I don't know where he is."

"He's fine," Dorothy reassured her. "He's just drunk. Now you have to decide if you want him back. He's going to call you tomorrow."

Serrita looked at Dorothy with a big smile washed with tears. She didn't question what Dorothy said. She sipped her soda and asked about Justine, Dorothy's newest arrival.

In the following years all that Appolonia had foretold came to pass. Dorothy's marriage to Richard ended two years after the birth of her third child, Paul. The majority of her sisters and brothers were aghast over the divorce, but over the years reason and good sense prevailed. Three years later Dorothy, a strong-willed mother with determination for her children and herself, married Bob Allison, a contracting engineer. Together they moved away from all the surroundings and hardships associated with Dorothy's early years to Nutley, New Jersey, a quiet neighborhood community north of where Dorothy was born.

Chapter 3

Sunday, December 3, 1967, 5:56 A.M.,
Nutley, New Jersey

The first glimmer of morning, like the onset of first dreams, was just discernible in the cloudy sky. And just as dreams give way before the impression of a new day, so the brilliance of the stars yielded to the light of the sun.

In her bed Dorothy stirred under the blankets. Her whole body moved, doubling over, then straightening and quieting. Her breathing was heavy; muttered words escaped her lips in half whispers. Thought and energy, images and reactions, swirled in a strange mental dance.

The sequence of fragmented pictures now pulsating through her consciousness had a force and life unlike most dreams. At first a shock of light glared in her vision. As the brilliant illumination diminished, an image of a small boy began to pulsate through.

"A little boy," she whispered. "Oh, my God, it's a little boy." He faded into the light. Her forehead wrinkled from the intensity of the illumination.

Once again the light began to change: first into a yellow brightness, then swirling into a cloudiness, a murkiness. The yellow gave way to the boy's image.

She saw his face, the face of a beautiful child, but with an unnatural, eerie pallor. Slowly the image floated toward her, moving in a stream of deep blue water. His flesh glistened. A haunting light was reflected in the boy's face.

"Eyes. I see his eyes," Dorothy cried. And his hands, clasped in front of him, looked black, as if charred.

In slow motion the little boy floated in her consciousness, without gravitation or weight. The blue liquid oozed and bubbled, then it quieted for a moment, only to gush forth with a force that caused Dorothy to writhe.

"His shoes are on the wrong feet. Poor child," she groaned. "Water. It's water. He's drowning," she half screamed. Her stomach and pelvis bolted forward.

The little body flashed before her: his flat blond hair was parted far over on the right side; she saw his green snowsuit, striped shirt, and a religious medal pinned underneath; his tiny shoes were on the wrong feet.

"My God. Who are you? Answer me, dear God," she pleaded. "Tell me where I can find you?" She heaved uncontrollably.

Faces of children populated her vision. Her grandchildren, her children, nieces, nephews, little boys, girls, strangers, faces familiar, faces unknown.

Who is this child? echoed through her mind. She strained to face the child, thinking that identifying him might prevent something from happening.

In desperation she willed her being in search of the child. With spiritlike speed she passed down a dark street, rain pouring all around. Warehouses loomed on the side. Gold letters flashed before her from the front of a building. She moved forward effortlessly, following some instinct, some power that propelled her into movement that was neither walking, nor running, nor flying, but sheer motion.

She passed piles of lumber stacked high in the darkness. A school. The number eight appeared. She glided beside the school building. A large cyclone fence glistened in the rain, surrounding the school yard. Behind the school, behind the fence, she came to a precipice.

The rain washed down the hill. The boy, she felt, was down below in the darkness. Down the hill she made her

way over three large slats of wood and through dense underbrush.

Through the pitch, rain glistened on the water. "The boy
is in the water," she gasped. She felt a rushing in her body;
she felt the darkness, the vastness.

Water was everywhere. Dorothy's body was soaked. She
saw the child's dead body passing freely through pipes. She
felt him inside her.

Suddenly he stopped. Solid. Stuck. Dorothy's pelvis
moved. She tried to help him, straining to relieve him. He
wouldn't budge. Her forehead tightened, her temples
throbbed. Electricity raced eellike through her being; water
rushed around the boy. She groaned loudly.

In an instant the waters swirled backward, and the body
receded into the darkness, disappearing totally in the wide
cavernous darkness of a pipe.

The images flowed in her mind. For an uncontrollable
instant Dorothy was suspended in space as she rode between two worlds; she was seeing and recording the images, and beginning to realize their significance at the same
time.

Dorothy's eyes opened. Her breathing was rough. She
put her hand on her stomach; her abdomen was tight with
pain. Her flannel nightgown stuck to her wet body. She sat
up at the side of her bed.

"Dreams . . . I've had dreams, but dear Lord, this is
incredible." The image of the little boy beat strongly
through her temples. Her right eye throbbed mercilessly.
"Who is he? Where is he?" She pushed at her husband.
"Wake up!"

Her husband's eyes barely opened. He exhibited little
awareness of the world.

"Listen," Dorothy pleaded. "I just had a dream. I think
I can help this kid," she said.

Dorothy ran to her dresser and jotted down on a piece
of paper, "6:00 A.M. Nightmare," and underlined it several
times. Next she went to the bathroom, washed her face
with warm water, and massaged her temples. Her head
pounded.

She looked in the mirror. "Oh, my God," she screamed.
"Look at my eye!" Her right eye was a deep bloody red.

"This has never happened before," she yelled at her husband. "I'm telling you, something is going on here. My eye is bleeding, and some kid is drowning."

"You're just having a dream," her husband mumbled.

"You're wrong. I am telling you now that you're wrong. I know I've had dreams before, but this one is somehow part of me. I can't explain it, but I know this is different. If I can get to the park, I can help the kid."

"Dorothy," her husband mumbled, "it's only six in the morning. People will think you're crazy. You aren't making much sense."

Dorothy sat on the edge of the bed. "This is what I saw. Listen to my dream." She wrapped herself in a blanket, took a deep breath, and recounted her dream. As she recalled the ghastly, haunting image of the little boy, she cried.

"I know I can help him, save him. I should go to the park," she implored.

"Dorothy, do you know which park?" Bob asked.

"No, I'm not even sure it is a park. But there's no place in this area that has trees like that except for a park."

The thought suddenly occurred to Dorothy that it was possible her dream was not local, that the boy was a total stranger. She knew, however, that he was real. His identity was the mystery.

Not since the death of her father, more than twenty years before, had she suffered a vision with such physical intensity. This vision, however, ran deeper through her being, emanating from a source never before felt, a place in her body she had never before detected. Only in labor had she felt such physical intensity and pain. Never before had the connection between her dreams and her body been one: what she saw, she felt.

She looked at her husband. He was asleep. She pulled on her robe and went downstairs to the kitchen. It was still dark outside, and a cold morning rain pelted against the window. She had thought it was going to be a clear day.

Dorothy felt that some explanation might be achieved astrologically. In the early fifties, she had discovered the world of astrology from drugstore periodicals. She soon

33

read and absorbed many books on the subject, becoming a fine, highly regarded astrologer.

In her Eighth House, known as the House of Death, Saturn (or Father Time) and Scorpio ruled supreme. The influence of the two stars gave her the extraordinary ability to sense death in any time period whether past, present, or future.

The child inside Dorothy cried out for help. She saw him floating somewhere, but did he drown yesterday, did she see it as it happened, or would he drown tomorrow, and could she prevent it? Her heart battled with the deep frustration and total helplessness that overwhelmed her.

A child. She had raised three children, done everything possible, often battling obstacles with superhuman energy and tenacity, to give them the advantages she never had as a child. She looked around her kitchen; it contained as much space as her brothers had had in the bedroom they all shared, and she felt rich in her own way, having a house in Nutley, New Jersey, with a yard in front and back, with a garage and with neighbors who had chosen the quiet, green community for its charm.

She wanted desperately to find the little boy and protect him. Tears came to her eyes as she thought of the little boy's mother, crying somewhere in fear that her son had disappeared, perhaps never to be found.

The clock over the refrigerator read 7:00. One hour had passed since her vision. Her body ached from the tension; she was exhausted. Soon Justine and Paul would awaken, and she would have to decide whether or not to pursue her vision.

She opened the refrigerator, pulled out a bowl of pancake batter, slid it across the counter toward the stove, and removed the orange-juice bottle, shaking it up and down. As she filled the kettle with water for coffee, she again saw the blond-haired boy, his blue eyes reaching out to her as if he were still vibrantly alive.

She called her brother, Tony. Tony was a skeptic. He did not adhere to Dorothy's astrological beliefs; nor could he explain her knack of predicting the future. But they had been very close as children, and Dorothy respected their differences, making sure her charts were off the dining-room table when Tony and his wife came to visit.

"This is different, Tony," she told him. "A kid's life is at stake. I've got to find out who the little boy is."

"Dorothy," Tony's strong but gentle voice began, "listen to me. You can't figure on knowing who the kid is. He might be thousands of miles from here, or he could be a combination of several kids you've seen lately. He could be someone you passed at the store." His voice got louder. "If he's real, he could be anyone and anyplace!"

"You're wrong!" Dorothy snapped. "Tony, answer me this. Why did my eye blow up and why does my stomach feel like I ate lead?"

"It may be some time before you find out his identity. You're going to have to relax until then."

"Relax?" Dorothy shrieked. "Me relax? When I got a house to run? And people floating around in my brain? How am I supposed to relax?"

Tony tried to assuage her. "You've been having dreams for years. Maybe not quite like this one, true," he hesitated for a second. "But you've had enough of these psychic experiences in your lifetime to know that answers don't come easy."

"Psychic? Is that what I am? You're smarter than I am, tell me if there are psychic doctors who can help me?" Dorothy pursued the word, tumbling it around in her mind, wondering what exactly it meant to "be psychic."

"I really don't know. I can't tell you because I've never met any psychics. Sometimes they show up on Johnny Carson's show," Tony's voice was teasing. "If I hear about any lost little boys, I'll call you right away. Okay?"

Dorothy put the phone down without hearing Tony's last words. The word "psychic" reverberated in her mind. She knew that Uranus, planet of intuition and the unexpected, ruled the world of the psychic, and that the remote star was high in her aspects. Now, it seemed, the time had come for Uranus, in the Twelfth House of Private Matters, to connect with Karma, their union bringing to a peak her visionary experience. As interpretation, Dorothy felt it was sound, and this helped her to accept the extraordinary phenomenon. Somehow, in astrological terms, she grappled with the notion that she was unique among men and women in the world.

"Mother!" Justine, Dorothy's sixteen-year-old daughter, suddenly stood before her. "What in God's name happened to your eye? Are you all right?"

Justine sat at her mother's side and held fast to her hand.

"I've had an awful night," Dorothy said. "But I'm okay. I'm just tired. I'm going to call the eye doctor and find out what this is about," she reassured Justine. "It really doesn't hurt. It just looks sinful."

Dorothy looked at her daughter who was taller than herself and had the eyes of her own mother. She was appreciative of her concern, but she didn't want to upset her.

"Is there anything I can do, Ma?" Justine asked.

"Make sure your brother wears rubbers. It's raining outside," Dorothy instructed her daughter.

"No, it's not raining anymore, Ma," fourteen-year-old Paul bellowed from the kitchen, overhearing their conversation.

"It's not raining?" Dorothy inquired. "Well, that's good news." If it clears, Dorothy thought to herself, I can walk down to the park and see if the kid is there.

Dorothy never went to the park that day. The entire day she stayed home, depressed and confused. The child's image haunted her. She made a few phone calls, checking those relatives and neighbors who had children the age of her little victim. Everything in her immediate society seemed totally in order: no children were missing.

For one month Dorothy questioned family, friends, and people who came over to have their charts read. Her vigilance was constant. Often she awakened in the early morning hours, her stomach knotted and cramped, the boy's image in her sight, her jaw clamped down, smashing her molars against each other as she tried to relieve the little boy and allow him to move. Already many years of subconscious but powerful dreams had severely damaged her jawbone. Eventually she would have to undergo several operations to build up the bone and muscle that had deteriorated from stress.

The boy, however, remained stuck. As Dorothy vacuumed the living room a few days later, she was suddenly struck by a stomach cramp. She sat down to catch her breath.

The image of the little boy came to life before her. His body moved in a solid, tightly bound manner, as if it had been preserved in a gel. Slowly, bathed in an eerie blue silence, he gyrated in circles, as if being drawn backward by an invisible force.

Her stomach ached. She pounded her jaw tightly and suddenly loosened it again. The boy moved through the water freely. He moved, he turned, he glided through her consciousness. What seemed like miles of movement wisped quickly through her mind. Seconds later the comet figure stopped abruptly. He was stuck again.

"Oh, no," she cried. "Not again. What can I do for this poor little boy? How can I help him?"

Dorothy climbed upstairs to wash her face and calm down. She had resolved to seek help.

Nutley, New Jersey, is a conservative, tucked-away community twenty-five minutes from Manhattan's George Washington Bridge. It is one of many towns in northern New Jersey to which ethnic families have escaped from the density of their early ghettos. It is predominantly Italian, Irish, and German.

The town's most evident landmarks are the enormous office compounds of two gigantic companies: pharmaceutical giant Hoffman La Roche and the defense research division of ITT.

Apart from the encircling highways and the two industries, Nutley is a quiet, green community. In its center is Booth Park, which meanders through the heart of the community neighborhoods. Approximately a hundred yards wide, Booth Park is five miles of serpentine land, with a lively stream running through its center. Little Japanese footbridges mark its path. The stream branches out in several places, disappearing underground through an intricate system of pipes, all running under various parts of the ITT complex and finally coming together at a point known as Bleachery Pond, which is in the adjoining town of Clifton, directly across the highway from ITT. From here, water pours into the Passaic River, eventually finding its way into Newark Bay and the grand Hudson River.

For the Nutley Police Department, the highways and water systems pose many problems. Closed in on all sides by neighboring towns, Nutley receives the bodies of victims who happen to have been disposed of in the New Jersey rivers that flow through the towns. The Nutley police are often relieved that Bleachery Pond is in Clifton's jurisdiction, for people often use it as a dumping ground for everything from dead animals to barrels to ordinary trash.

Chief Francis Buel, Nutley's chief of police, had worked eighteen years in the Nutley Police Department. Chief Buel liked order and sameness; in the eyes of his men his German heritage and his attitude toward people were closely linked.

A large, red-haired man, Chief Buel received Dorothy Allison cordially. It was January 3, 1968, and he was feeling tolerant in these first days of the new year.

Patrolman Don "Vic" Vicaro led the short woman into the chief's office. Dorothy wore a blue polyester suit. Her brown hair was in beauty-parlor order, still giving off the scent of that morning's hair spray. Her eyes did little to hide the fear she had been living with for a month. She knew in her heart that what she was about to do was going to change her life irrevocably.

Left alone, Dorothy and the chief looked at one another. He sat behind his large, official Danish-Modern desk.

"Now, Mrs. Allison, what can the Nutley Police Department do for you? I trust nothing serious has happened?"

"No, everything is fine with me, I guess. It's just this kid I think has drowned, and I wonder if you might have heard about it."

"Did you see this child drown, Mrs. Allison?" The chief sat up in his large, padded chair.

"No, not exactly. I saw it, but not officially." Dorothy considered the best way to impart what she was trying to say.

"Did you or didn't you see a child drown?" the chief was trying to understand.

"I did. In my dreams. Or rather, in a vision," she stammered.

38

The chief's light red brows rose. "In a dream, you say? Do you often have dreams of this nature, Mrs. Allison?"

"No, not too often. I've had some incredible dreams in my lifetime, but not too many that I discovered to be real," she explained.

The chief looked at Dorothy. She seemed to be perfectly rational, though nervous and slightly excited.

"You mean you are psychic, right?" the chief asked.

Dorothy sighed. "I guess so," she said reluctantly, never having discussed anything of that nature with a stranger.

"I haven't had a moment's peace in a month," Dorothy began. "I saw this kid drown on December third, at six in the morning. I wrote it down when I woke up. Never before have I had a dream like that. It was so real that I felt it through my body. My right eye exploded and I had to wear sunglasses till last week."

"Exploded?" the chief asked.

"The doctor said a blood vessel broke from tension. The tension was the kid drowning, I tell you."

"What would you like me to do, Mrs. Allison?"

"Maybe you'd recognize the description of the little boy. Not you personally, of course, but maybe someone in the department knows about a missing kid."

"Mrs. Allison—" the chief began.

"Call me Dorothy, please," she interrupted.

"Dorothy, I want you to tell me about the little boy. Describe to me what you are seeing."

Dorothy wondered if his attentiveness meant that he believed in her ability to see, that he believed in psychics. She did not want him to think she was a crazy woman wandering in from the street.

She took a deep breath and her expression relaxed as if she had temporarily gone inside, like a snail, to find something. Her voice had a distant quality to it, though she looked directly at the chief.

"I see a little boy. Maybe five or six years old. It's hard to tell. He has blond hair and it's parted far over on one side, not like most kids. I see his poor little body in the water. His shoes are on the wrong feet and he's wearing a green snowsuit and a religious medal on his shirt. His hands are clasped together, and I don't know what could have happened, but they look black, like they've been burned."

"Where is this boy?" Chief Buel whispered.

"In a pipe somewhere, like a sewer pipe. He's stuck. I think the pipe must be in a park, because I see some trees and a school."

Chief Buel sat back, absorbing the barrage of facts. He mentally scanned the latest reports and records regarding missing or murdered children. He must have had a gnawing feeling that the child Dorothy described might indeed be a little boy who was missing in Nutley.

"Chief Buel, the kid has got to be somewhere and maybe if you find this pipe he's in, you'll find him," she challenged him. "The pipe looks broken or crooked. I can't tell, really."

Chief Buel stood up. "Wait here a moment, Dorothy. I'll be right back." And his large frame exited through the door.

"Get me the missing-persons file," he said to his assistant, "dating back two months, I'd say."

Patrolman Vicaro asked the chief about the woman he showed into his office.

"Why? Do you know her?" the Chief asked.

"Not really. I saw her come in. She looked interesting, that's all," the officer replied. "Is she missing someone?" he inquired, pointing to the missing-persons file being handed the chief.

"No more than a few loose screws," the chief snarled. "She hasn't lost anyone. In fact, she's found someone. She thinks she's found a little kid who we might be missing. A kid who drowned, she says."

Vicaro's curiosity was piqued. "Hey, we lost a kid about a month ago, and we never found him. Remember three times into the stream in Booth Park in freezing cold weather? The kid who was playing with his brother . . ."

"Wait! I do remember," the chief's eyes brightened. "Get me the file and come into my office. Don't mention anything about this case in front of the woman. We'll see how much she can tell us first," he instructed the patrolman.

Patrolman Vicaro looked the part of an Italian crooner,

with his salt-and-pepper hair combed straight back, his gravelly tobacco-laden voice, a blue star-sapphire pinky ring, and a pack of cigarettes neatly tucked in his socks. Raised in a house of four families, he had become a cop in 1954 after serving in the army, a time when being a cop meant elevating oneself to first-class citizenship.

As a kid Vic had seen movies in which hypnosis had been used, and it had stimulated his fantasies. He sensed the mind was a wonderous machine, and that hypnosis might be the key to it. That curiosity was heightened while serving in the army, when he saw a stage show in which hypnosis was performed on members of the audience.

One day, after he had left the service, he was walking around New York City when a book on hypnosis caught his eye in a shop window. He bought the book, read the entire thing that night, and the next day practiced on his brother.

When Vic left the service, the country's economic situation was not good. His trade had been laying carpets and tile floors, and he had hoped to expand it into a business of his own. But the economy did not allow for people without financial means to begin businesses. His father, who had come to the United States from Italy when he was two, had been a laborer all his life, working his way into the society and gaining the respect of others.

When Vic's post-army alternatives looked slim, it was his father who suggested he go into police work. Reluctant to don another uniform, Vicaro took the exams anyway and passed. He was a patrolman.

Chief Buel reentered the office.

"When is your birthday?" Dorothy asked him.

"My birthday?" the chief repeated as if a difficult question had been posed. "Well, my birthday is August third."

"Ah! A Leo," Dorothy pronounced. "I'll have to be careful," she said. She wondered if asking him the time of his birth would be too brazen. The thought was interrupted by the arrival of Patrolman Vicaro.

In the next half hour Dorothy recataloged the details of her vision, giving the chief and Vicaro a chance to mentally compare notes with the case they had on hand.

Vicaro queried Dorothy about various aspects of her life

and her familiarity with Nutley. He discovered through brief interrogation that she did not know the Kurscics family, the surname of the drowned five-year-old on file, nor was she at all familiar with the Kurscics's neighborhood, or Booth Park for that matter. Vic was surprised Dorothy had never actually been in Booth Park, the largest, most attractive land area in the town.

"My kids always play around the corner at Nicholas Park. We're a one-car family," she explained.

When she heard the name "Kurscics," she simply asked, "Is that the little boy's last name?"

Chief Buel explained that, yes, one of their missing cases was a little Polish boy named Michael Kurscics. That was all they told Dorothy at that time.

Twenty minutes later Chief Buel, Dorothy, and Vicaro were driving in a police car, while two policemen followed in another car: Buel's escape car.

Dorothy's heart halted in mid-pulse when the patrolman sitting in the front seat turned to her and asked, "Have you ever been hypnotized?"

"No, I never have," she gasped. "I don't think I've ever wanted to be hypnotized, either."

The policeman saw she was frightened. "It's really nothing," he told her. "If I know how to hypnotize people, it can't be too difficult. I went to school to learn to use hypnotism in police work. We use it all the time," he lied.

"You do?" Dorothy wanted reassurance. She was surprised that hypnotism was used in Nutley.

"Oh, sure. It helps people remember things they might otherwise think they forgot. Like where the little boy's body is right now."

Chief Buel interrupted at this point, not sure he wanted his cop to hypnotize Dorothy. Never having worked with a psychic before, he might not have been comfortable with what he might find in her mind. However, he admitted to himself that he had seen some interesting work done with hypnosis, and Dorothy's description did sound too close for comfort.

"Mrs. Allison," Chief Buel said. "I assure you that hypnosis is a routine affair and not harmful. Perhaps if Vicaro hypnotizes you right here in the car, you might be able to direct us to Michael Kurscics's body."

Dorothy's mind reeled with images of levitation from the *Ed Sullivan Show*, and sleepwalking horrors from films and television. "But these are the police," she thought to herself. "If I can't trust them, who can I trust?"

"You want to hypnotize me right here in the car?" she asked.

"If that's okay with you," Chief Buel said.

"Sure," Dorothy finally agreed.

Buel looked at his watch. "It's twelve-thirty now. Why don't you tell some of the men to go on to lunch," he said to the policeman driving the car. "I'll hang around for another couple of minutes to see what comes up. Otherwise I'll be back at the station around one-thirty."

Vicaro switched places with Chief Buel, and Dorothy leaned on the door, stretching her short legs on the floor. She tried to seem calm, wanting to help the police in understanding her dream. If hypnosis would bring them closer to a solution, then she would participate, in spite of her fears.

Within minutes the patrolman had relaxed her into a deep trance. Her nervous breathing was now quieter, as if an inner metronome had changed tempo for slower music. Her head rested against the window.

"What do you see, Dorothy?" he asked.

"An old broken-down house on a huge empty lot. No one is living in it. There's a "No Trespassing" sign on the door."

"You mean the old shack across the highway?"

"Yeah, the one we call the haunted house."

They drove on and parked beside a large, empty lot where the last house stood in an area that would soon be developed for shopping. It was now blanketed in snow. The windows of the two-story wooden structure were boarded up, and the porch looked dilapidated.

"Is Michael Kurscics's body near here, Dorothy?" inquired Vicaro.

"No, not now," she replied. He began to wonder where this might lead them. "What do you see now?"

"I see a room full of books and papers all over a big

43

desk. There's a tall blond woman walking back and forth, like she's waiting for someone. She lives between two cemeteries . . ."

"Dorothy, wait a minute. I think you're picking up things from the area that have nothing to do with the kid. Let's move to another area," Vicaro suggested.

Chief Buel motioned to Vicaro. "I'm leaving," he said. Then in a low voice, "You better know what you're doing. I'm leaving her in your hands. Let me know if anything comes up."

Chief Buel drove away with one of his men. He must have wondered about this woman who seemed such a bundle of energy and nerves, seeing a little kid drown and then coming to the police with the information. He must not have felt comfortable working with a psychic, if indeed she proved to be psychic. He had not built his reputation on being lenient and liberal, and was not sure he wanted his name associated with the woman.

Vicaro was feeling frustrated. "Let's go to the place where we know the kid drowned," he said to the driver. "Maybe you're not seeing things right," he suggested to Dorothy.

Dorothy was hurt by the questioning.

Several minutes later they parked near the beginning of Booth Park, fifty feet from the bridge Michael and Pat Kurscics had played on that drizzly December 3 Sunday morning—the morning of Dorothy's dream. It was here that the police had begun their search, dragging the water which two miles downstream emptied into the Passaic River. The Nutley police had been aided by the Essex County Park Police, including a pair of skin divers, in a day-long search of the river. Assisting in the search were volunteers of the Nutley First Aid Squad and Civil Defense group. All these men together had found nothing in the swollen river, whose current they clocked at faster than thirty miles. Even the paint can, which seven-year-old Pat Kurscics reported had lured his younger brother to the edge of the water, had disappeared.

Dorothy knew none of these facts.

Vicaro once again put Dorothy under hypnotic trance. "Okay, can you hear me, Dorothy?" he questioned.

"Yes, loud and clear," she confirmed.

"Describe Michael Kurscics to me, if you can."

Dorothy squinted as if a bright light confronted her.

"I see him. Oh my God, he looks so still and dead. There's a light around his body. He's not moving right now. He's stuck in the pipe."

"Is he stuck right here, near the bridge?" the officer pursued.

"No, I don't see the bridge. I see the school and a broken pipe. A crooked pipe. At least it looks broken."

Vicaro brought her out of the trance. He decided that enough had been done for one day, and she obviously wasn't going to find the boy that day. Something, he felt, had to be done to clear her vision.

"Are there any broken pipes that you know of in the park?" Dorothy asked the patrolman.

"Not that I know of, but I'll have it checked out. Maybe the chief will know."

When Dorothy and Vicaro appeared in the police parking lot, she felt weary and cold. The temperature had dropped below freezing and her feet were frozen.

Vicaro turned to her. "Do you mind if I give you a call later, or drop by your house? Maybe we could try again tomorrow, or whenever it's convenient for you."

"Sure. Let me know what time you boys want to come by and I'll fix you lunch. How's that?"

Vicaro smiled to himself. It's hard to think that this little lady is making all this up, he thought.

"You get some rest, and maybe we'll find the kid's body tomorrow. I think you know where he is," Vicaro concluded.

Dorothy was pleased to hear him confirm his belief in her dream. Sharing it seemed to ease the burden, but she was still frightened for the child. More than fear, she felt a constant sadness. Sadness for a boy she did not know, whose family had meant nothing to her before December 3, and whose death still haunted her daily existence. She had a gnawing feeling that if she had acted upon her dream a month earlier, the boy might have been saved. Then again, there was the chance that her dream had nothing to do with Michael Kurscics, at all.

"Why me?" she asked herself as she drove past the large Hoffman La Roche complex of buildings, known locally as the "Pill Box." "Why did *I* dream about this kid when there're all these people around who might have recognized him?" The ghastly image in her mind would not budge from its place, wherever that place might be.

She was stymied by the little bridge where Vicaro told her the child had drowned. She had no picture of that place in her mind. Nowhere in her dreams had she seen the little footbridge. Nor did she recognize the surrounding area. The scene of her dreams did not resemble any spot she had seen in the park that day.

Chief Buel, listening to Vicaro's report, wondered about the same points. "Where do you suppose she's seeing the kid?" he asked the patrolman. "Or do you think she's seeing this kid at all?"

"I don't know. I really can't make out what she's talking about. How could the kid get up around the haunted house if he fell into the stream? There isn't a stream next to the house," Vicaro said.

"I think the kid's in the Passaic, to tell you the goddamned truth. The kid drowned thirty days ago in fast-moving water." Chief Buel shook his head slowly. "I'll bet he won't be washed up till spring, and by that time, there won't be anything left to bury but a religious medal."

Vicaro thought for a moment. The religious medal was in Dorothy's description, not in the Kurscics's description. The chief was integrating Dorothy's facts, as well.

"I'd like a few days to work with the woman. With another couple of days of hypnosis, I figure I can find out all she's got to say. I'd like to walk her through the park to see if she gets any strong feelings."

"I don't know," the chief looked perplexed. "I'm afraid she might be a waste of time."

The phone rang. Chief Buel picked it up.

"Yeah? Mrs. Who?" He cupped his hand over the phone. "It's your lady, Vic."

"What can I do for you, Mrs. Allison? Yes, I mean Dorothy."

"One moment. Let me ask Vicaro here. Maybe he'll know." Once again he cupped the receiver. "She wants to know if she can talk to the kid's mother. She thinks that hearing her voice and meeting her will help her find the kid."

"The kid's mother isn't in the area right now. I'll try and find her, but I don't think she's around."

"Dorothy," the chief piped into the phone, "the patrolman here says he'll find you the kid's mother. He's not exactly sure where she is right now, but he'll get on it right away." He hesitated for a moment. "No, I don't think she's on vacation. What's that? You say there's a crooked pipe in the park? I'll ask Vicaro about it. Thank you, Mrs. Allison."

"That woman needs something, and I don't know what it is, either," the chief muttered, dropping the receiver. "Or maybe I do know," he smiled. "Okay, Vicaro, you can spend some time on this case. If you don't find anything by Friday, though, you'll have to use your own time." He looked out the window. "You're going to have a rough time finding anything in this cold weather. It's supposed to snow again tomorrow. If that kid is in ice, there ain't a cop this side of Manhattan that'll find him. Unless he's a seal."

"Okay, Chief, as you say." Vicaro thought for a moment. "What do you think about using a real doctor to hypnotize her? She makes me nervous. I never messed with a psychic before."

"You really think something is there, don't you?" The chief looked Vicaro in the eyes. "You believe in this, don't you?"

"What do you want me to say, Chief?" Vicaro lashed out defensively. "This little woman walks in and describes almost exactly a kid we've been missing for a month, and she's never even heard of the family. I think we should do anything we can to find this kid."

"I don't see the kid's parents knocking down our doors, either. We slopped through every foot of freezing water in the park and you're telling me we've done nothing? You want to drag that goddamned stream again in all this ice and find the same crap? If you do, you're welcome to do it on your own time. Okay?"

"Sorry, Chief," Vicaro said in a quieter tone of voice.

"Find out who the city cops are using for hypnosis.

There're some big people in New York. Just don't tell the other cops that this woman is a psychic. Hear me?"

"Great." Vicaro was relieved. "See you later, Chief," Vicaro closed the door behind him.

Chief Buel sat for a quiet moment. Suddenly he remembered Dorothy's mentioning a crooked pipe in the park. He picked up his phone and buzzed his assistant.

"When Vicaro comes back, tell him I want him to get the underground map of Booth Park from the city engineer's office. I want him to find out if there's anything in the park that's crooked."

At home that evening Dorothy pondered the day's events as she finished washing the dinner dishes and straightening her kitchen. The police seemed nice enough, but she did not trust them completely. How many people come into the police department like I did today? she wondered. Probably not many. I wonder how my chart reads for tomorrow. I have a feeling I'm going to find that kid . . . I know it's Michael Kurscics. I really just know that. "I don't know how in God's name I know that," she said to the dishes, "but I do."

Her thoughts were interrupted by the ringing of the phone. Patrolman Vicaro was calling.

Vicaro asked Dorothy if she would be available the next afternoon for another spin in the park. "I'd like to try hypnosis one more time. And then, I have a suggestion," he said. "I'd like to take you to a real doctor in New York for hypnosis and interrogation. They have doctors in the city who do this kind of thing all the time," he explained. "I got the name of one of the biggest. The New York City cops use him all the time. Why don't you think about it tonight and you can let me know tomorrow when I pick you up. How's that?"

Dorothy was pleased by the call. It somehow made her feel important. "Terrific. Come by anytime. I'll be here all day, except when I take my kids to school. Did you find out if that park has crooked pipes?"

"Chief Buel and the city engineer say there ain't none. They should know. Both of them were there when the park was laid out, too."

48

The image of the little boy stuck in the crooked pipe flashed before her, as a television picture struggles to focus. "I know there's a crooked pipe somewhere. That kid is stuck there."

"The chief says if you pick out where you feel this pipe is, he'll dig it out. How's that?"

"You tell the chief I love him." Dorothy's elation was evident. "See you tomorrow, Vic."

For the next few weeks Vicaro and Dorothy tried to locate the child's body by traveling through the area and walking endlessly through Booth Park. Through snow and slush Dorothy plodded on in her efforts to resolve the vision.

Vicaro had a copy of the city engineer's map of Booth Park and its environs.

"As far as I can tell, Dorothy, there's nothing in the park that's crooked or bent," he explained to her as she looked over the map, seeing nothing but squiggles and lines.

"There are places like this," his finger pointed to a place where two lines met at perpendiculars, one line meeting the main pipe line. "But," Vicaro continued, "nothing can get stuck at these points. Too big and too much flow."

"Well," Dorothy thought, "I don't understand it either."

"Why don't we go ahead and see if you feel anything as we walk through the park. Chief Buel did say he would dig anywhere you pointed."

It was not until two days later that Dorothy, Vicaro, and another policeman put the chief's promise into action.

Dorothy walked ahead of the two policemen who were talking about cases she did not want to hear about, for fear her concentration would be interrupted. In her hypnotic state, she sensed the closeness of something. The image of the boy was constant in her vision.

Her feet moved slowly as she made fresh tracks in the snow. She turned to Vicaro with a finger extended downward.

"Here," she called excitedly. "I feel it. I think there's a crooked pipe down there."

The two policemen looked at the spot Dorothy designated. Nothing unusual was evident aboveground. The terrain did not alter drastically.

Vicaro went to his car radio and called for help. While waiting for the arrival of the digging crew, the three figures sat in the car, where warmth revived them.

An hour later, anyone passing Booth Park might have thought that a film crew was at work. Tremendous high-intensity lights illuminated the area Dorothy had pinpointed, brightly reflected in the snow and frozen soil.

A crew of six men began digging around 3:30 P.M. It was dark and cold already. They picked their way through several feet of mud and rock.

Two hours had passed when Chief Buel stopped by on his way home. He found Dorothy administering coffee and doughnuts to his men. He smiled at the sight of the small woman rendering care as if to the wounded, bolstering their cold and weary spirits, bouncing around to see what progress was being made.

"Your men are so beautiful," Dorothy ran up to the chief. "They've been working for over two hours now, and I think we're getting closer every minute." Dorothy was feeling anxious about putting so many people to work in such cold weather, all due to her vision.

As the two stood talking, one of the men standing in the trench called out to them. "Over here. I bet this is what you're talking about."

Dorothy ran over to the man. There, in front of his boots, was a large, round, broken pipe. The cold weather had worked its way through the seam, causing it to crack. Movement in the soil below had pushed a section of it up, causing it to jut out several inches like a broken jaw.

Chief Buel looked down. "A five-year-old body could get stuck in a snag like that." He looked at Dorothy. "The city engineer will be surprised to know he has a crooked pipe in Booth Park."

"We're getting closer," Vicaro said. "There's no body here now. You'll find that kid soon, I bet," he said with assurance to Dorothy and the chief.

Dorothy looked tired. "Let's call it a day, okay?" Vicaro suggested. He and the chief escorted Dorothy across the field.

"Those boys must be hungry now," she said to Vicaro. "How about my fixing you and the boys an Italian dinner at my house?"

Later that evening, when Vicaro was leaving Dorothy's feast, he told her that he would take her to New York City on Saturday for a session with a doctor.

"What kind of doctor?" Dorothy wanted to know.

"What do you mean, what kind of doctor?" Vicaro kidded her. "A shrink!" he exclaimed. "You know, a psychiatrist."

"Oh, Holy God above, now a psychiatrist! What will my family say now?" she moaned, half enjoying the drama, and definitely intrigued by the notion of a psychiatrist.

"What time?" Dorothy inquired. "Do shrinks get up early on Saturdays?"

"How'm I supposed to know," Vicaro jested. "I told him we'd be there around eleven. How's that with you?"

"That's just dandy with me. The earlier the better. I got a ton of shopping to do in the afternoon. You know something, Vic?" Dorothy's voice had suddenly softened and was almost contemplative. "Looking for a dead body is not the easiest work in the world. Nor the happiest." She clutched the gold medal on her chest with her fist. "As long as I've got my Saint Anthony with me, I'll never quit. I'm already seeing other things, other faces, and I know I won't be able to let go of them easily. I think I have my work cut out for me. We'll have to wait and see."

"I think you're onto something, Dorothy," the officer said. "I know it's not easy. And I hope we're right about this little boy."

"I know we're right," Dorothy said as she closed the door behind her. Thirty seconds later her head popped out the door again. "Hey, Vicaro," she hollered into the night. "Get me that baby's mother!" And she slammed the door.

The following Saturday morning, January 16, Dorothy was up early, cleaning the kitchen and preparing breakfast for her sleeping family. These were the times when she could think, reflect over events involving her children, and plan strategies she would set forth to her family when they descended for breakfast, too groggy to be resistant to an old pro like Dorothy.

"Not a very good day for a visit to the city," she thought out loud. Through the kitchen window the world was gray and cloudy; frozen remnants of snow were piled high against the house. Neighbors' Christmas lights still flickered in the trees.

Vicaro was supposed to pick her up at 10:00, and she still had a full list of errands and chores she wanted done. If Justine had time, she would delegate some chores to her. Dorothy did not believe in asking the men of her household to perform household duties.

"I'm going into New York today with the police," Dorothy said to Justine and Paul. "I don't know what time I'll be home, but I have a feeling it won't be till late this afternoon."

"Think you'll find the little boy today, Ma?" Justine asked.

"No," Dorothy said. "But I have a feeling some important stuff is going to happen. I'm not nervous with the hypnosis now, like I was before. I think I'll be able to see more with a real good doctor and hypnotist.

"Anyway," she handed one end of a curtain to Justine, and they began to fold them automatically, "Uranus is high in my Tenth House today, which is a good sign for mental powers. But I have to be careful about my natal Venus, which will definitely affect the whole mess."

"Are you sure this doctor knows what he's doing?" her husband asked. Bob knew his wife would do what she thought best, regardless of any advice or warnings anyone might offer.

"How'm I supposed to know?" Dorothy shrugged. "I never did this sort of thing before. God knows, no one in my family ever went to a psychiatrist. I still don't know exactly what they do."

Dorothy thought for a moment. "All New Yorkers are weird," she proclaimed. "But this doctor, or whatever he is, isn't charging me a penny, and I think that's terrific.

"He's going to help me figure out what I'm seeing, too," Dorothy went on. "That isn't easy. This morning, while I was cleaning the den, I kept having crazy flashes. First," she raised a finger dramatically, "I see pots and pans on a big wall in a huge kitchen, so I figure I got to get breakfast made. Then," she raised a second finger, "I see lots of people moving through the kitchen, like it's a restaurant." She raised both arms to the ceiling. "God save me if all those people ever set foot in my kitchen!"

Dorothy sat down and poured more coffee for her husband. "I see all these people going crazy, like someone is getting hurt," she continued. "Someone doubles over and hundreds of people pounce on him. Just as I'm getting close to focusing on faces, Michael Kurscics's face appears."

She sat back and took a deep breath. "I swear, there's no way all this doesn't add up to mean something. I just got to have help figuring it out."

Dorothy looked at the clock. "Oh my God, Vicaro will be here in an hour. I've got to get moving." She fingered her hair. "I'm running over to let Rosemary do something with this mop. I can't look this way for the doctor. Especially since he's not charging me."

Vicaro and Dorothy had spent at least a few hours daily looking for clues to the whereabouts of Michael Kurscics. She still had not met the boy's mother, who was reported to be living in another town at the time of her son's drowning. Vicaro promised he would find the mother for Dorothy the following week.

"I won't be able to find the kid till I meet her," Dorothy nudged. "I don't care what kind of woman she is, a mother is hurt when she loses a child."

When the doorbell rang, Dorothy registered a feeling of panic. What's going to happen today? she asked herself in the mirror, positioning her scarf and tying it securely under her chin. What a strange world this is.

When Dorothy opened the door, Patrolman Vicaro smiled. "Ready?"

She jumped forward and gave him a smack on the cheek and a quick hug. He returned the affectionate gesture, calming her nerves a bit.

"Hey," he stood back, "you look terrific. Is that a new coat?"

"Honey," she winked at the officer, "if not now, when?"

Vicaro smiled as the two drove off in the police car for Manhattan. Circling on the highway for entry into the Lincoln Tunnel, Dorothy looked out over Manhattan's skyline, gray against the winter skies. For much of her life she had seen the majestic city from the poor man's vantage point of Jersey City. She saw the city as a symbol of formidable strength.

"I love to come to New York City, but I'd never want to live there," she said to Vicaro. "It's a crazy place, isn't it?"

"Yeah, a lot of crime and dirt," Vicaro responded. Dorothy smiled at the policeman's response, realizing that his profession gave him a particular attitude toward New York.

As Dorothy looked out over the West Side, and at the ships docked alongside the piers, she felt anxious. She wasn't sure why, but she had an inkling that something she saw along the waterfront had some special significance.

They stopped in front of one of Central Park West's Art Deco triumphs, a building with an imposing brick and silver chrome facade.

"Isn't this something?" Dorothy admired the lights in the chrome of the entryway. Her fingers ran up the shiny surface. "And not a bit of dust, either," she nodded approvingly to the doorman.

When the correct apartment had been found, Vicaro pushed the buzzer. Seconds later a dark, curly haired man, well manicured and in his late thirties, opened the door.

"Hello, there, I'm Dr. Ribner." He extended his hand to Dorothy and Vicaro and led them into the vestibule.

"Please come right in. I'm so pleased to finally meet you, Mrs. Allison," he said. "Why don't we sit down for a moment, talk some business, and then I'd like to step outside with patrolman Vicaro so he can give me a quick rundown on the case." He looked at Dorothy. "I don't want you to be influenced by any details," he explained.

As Dorothy walked into the doctor's office, she admired the wall of dark-wood bookcases with glass doors jammed full of books and knickknacks from all over the world. A large blue and white Victorian urn stood on a bookcase.

"What do you use that for? It's too big for cookies." Dorothy asked with childlike curiosity.

"It's from my parents' home. Big enough to hide a kid, isn't it?" the doctor teased her.

Dr. Ribner escorted Dorothy to the seat in front of his gilded Empire desk. Vicaro sat next to her. Ribner assumed command from behind the desk.

"Dorothy, how are you feeling?" Ribner inquired softly.

"Nervous. Very scared, to be honest. I was hypnotized recently, for the first time, and I assure you, I was plenty frightened."

"I can appreciate that. But you don't need to be frightened now," he reassured her. "At least, not of hypnotism. I imagine your visions might be frightening, though."

"Yes, I can't begin to tell you. My whole life has not been the same since December third."

"We'll get into that in a moment." Dr. Ribner leaned forward. "I see your gifts are not only psychic, but that you are gifted with beauty, as well."

Dorothy felt her head pound. The vibrations are right, she thought to herself. This man is on my side. Much of her fear slipped away and she began to ease into her surroundings.

The doctor became serious. "To be honest, I don't exactly know what role hypnosis can play in helping you or anyone else understand what you're seeing. For the most part, psychic phenomena are outside the realm of scientific data and research. That is not to say that there isn't research going on, because there is. Not as much attention is being given to the workings of the mind as, let's say, physical diseases like cancer. But scientists—mostly physicists—have been trying to apply their branch of science to ESP, telepathy, and all the other varieties of parapsychological wonders."

He paused, looked into Vicaro's eyes, then Dorothy's, waiting for questions. When there were none, he concluded, "Just believing in it is the first and most important breakthrough to understanding."

Dorothy reached out and touched the doctor's hand. "I think I love you," she said. They all smiled. They all understood.

Dorothy looked around the room toward the only window, which offered a view of other buildings and a great expanse of New York winter sky. A large assortment of coleus and dark green snake plants cluttered the windowsill. Between the window and the desk stood a soft, yellow leather reclining chair. Dorothy gulped.

"That's right," Ribner smiled. "Every psychiatrist has a couch."

Dorothy smiled nervously. "Does every patient have a dream?" she asked.

"No," he replied.

"Good, then you won't mind working on one more."

"Dorothy, why don't you excuse Patrolman Vicaro and me for one moment. We'll step into the waiting room."

"Go right ahead. I'll sit right here and stare at this beautiful desk and rug," she looked down. "My God, it's so clean!" she exclaimed. "Don't you ever have patients with muddy feet?"

"Not many, I suppose," the doctor replied as he closed the outside door behind him.

Dorothy looked at the diplomas on the wall and thought about the Latin she had heard as a child. Latin meant church to Dorothy. Latin was everything she had been forced to learn by her mother and oldest sister as a youngster. Latin was the language she aspired to know so that she would be accepted, like everyone else in the church. Latin was the unintelligible language of God, the language that drifted from her mother's bedroom as she and her friends prayed in the afternoon. In the afternoon, Dorothy smiled to herself, so that my father wouldn't see them.

She sighed nervously. I had enough Latin to choke a horse when I was a kid.

"Okay, Dorothy," Dr. Ribner's voice interrupted. "Why don't you lie down on the couch and we'll proceed. I've asked the officer to remain outside while I hypnotize you, so that you aren't distracted. Later he will help me in the questioning."

Dorothy plopped into the reclining seat, her legs not quite making it to the end. She looked to her right and saw a small black rectangular box with two large dials on it. She read out loud, "Dose . . . Output . . . Frequency."

"This little machine helps you to focus your concentration," Dr. Ribner explained.

"I'm not mechanical, but if this little box can help me focus, I'll marry it," Dorothy announced.

"It's really very simple. What I'm going to do is prick your ear a tiny, tiny bit with this," and he held up a small clamp connected by one red and one white wire to the box, and touched it to his ear.

"What you will feel is no more than a slight run of electricity in the ear. We use this rather than an acupuncture needle."

"Don't explain it to me," Dorothy warned. "I get too nervous around doctors and needles."

"Do you have any questions?" Ribner asked as he pulled the window shade down, covering half the window.

"Nope. Let's get going."

The clamp was applied to Dorothy's ear, and soon she felt a slight buzz of electricity. "Now, I want you to think of the word *relax*. I want you to think about its meaning. Spell it out. Feel it. Just relax now," Ribner's voice was smooth and firm.

"Close your eyes and relax your body. Concentrate on the feelings in your ear and relax. Just relax."

Vicaro could barely hear muffled voices from the waiting area. His ear to the door, he strained to hear what was happening in the doctor's office. He wondered what methods the doctor used for hypnotizing. He felt embarrassed to discuss the topic. As he strained closer to the door, it opened and caught him by surprise.

"Step quietly," whispered Ribner. "She's perfectly fine. An easy subject."

The doctor sat directly in front of Dorothy, one arm on the windowsill. Vicaro sat next to the door, in front of the desk. He caught sight of the clamp connected to Dorothy's right ear and felt a shiver go up his spine. Brave lady, he couldn't help thinking.

"Dorothy, how do you feel?" the doctor began.

"Fine. I think."

"Do you know where you are?"

"Yes, with you."

"Okay, Dorothy, breathe easily for a moment and describe to me how you see Michael Kurscics."

Dorothy's heavy-lidded eyes appeared relaxed to the observer. Behind the eyelids, distance melted into nothingness, time lost its meaning. Images flickered before her as she reached for an image of Michael Kurscics.

"Michael Kurscics," the doctor repeated.

The image of the little boy, now dead six weeks, glimmered before her.

"I see him now," Dorothy's calm voice stated. "He looks awful. He's still stuck in the pipe. I don't know if it's the same place."

"Can you stand above the pipe?"

She paused as she realigned her vantage point.

"I see the pipe. I see the water rushing over the pipe and the little boy's body."

"Describe for me what you see above the pipe. What can you identify in the area?"

"I see snow. Tall trees with no leaves. There's a large square thing with blue in it. It looks painted, but it's meant to be water, I think."

"You mean the stream?" asked Ribner for clarification.

"No, this is different," Dorothy said.

"A swimming pool?" Vicaro interjected. "Do you see a swimming pool, Dorothy?"

"Yes. It's up on a hill."

Vicaro nodded his head approvingly to the doctor. He recognized the pool as the one directly above the spot where the little boy drowned.

"What happens to Michael Kurscics near the pool?" Ribner queried.

"I see him falling into the stream. He's poking around for something, a can of some sort, and he's falling as he reaches out for the stupid can. It's slippery and cold. The water is very cold. It stuns him, shocks him."

"Is he there now, Dorothy?"

"No, he's stuck now. But he was there awhile ago."

"Where?"

"In the pipe."

"Which pipe? Where is the pipe?"

"Which pipe?" Dorothy repeated. "Well, I see ITT. I see a school. There's a lot of water, like a bigger river, or something. Bigger than the stream. And I see something poking out of the water, it looks like a chimney. Like a smokestack."

"Okay, Dorothy," Ribner stopped her. "You say you see the boy in a pipe. Right?"

"Right."

"Has he been in the same place for the whole time?"

Dorothy thought for a moment. "I don't think so. It's hard for me to say. I know I keep seeing him in different places, though."

Vicaro was trying hard to put all the landmarks together. It didn't make sense. Most of the time she was describing things along the path of Booth Park and the stream. But the haunted house was nowhere near that stream. Anyway, the stream had been searched several times and had produced no body and no pipe. Chief Buel's notion that the kid's body was somewhere in the Passaic or Hudson made more sense with every passing day.

Vicaro was beginning to sense that there was something strange about the sequence of Dorothy's visions. The spot she described in her first dream, on December 3, was yet to be found. Now, for the first time, she was seeing the beginning of the boy's accident. Was it because she had overheard details during the investigation? Because she had become familiar with Booth Park?

Vicaro sighed. I'll bet the kid she saw isn't Kurscics at all, he thought. Then a voice in him said, But what about the clothes and the timing?

Dr. Ribner was pleased with Dorothy's work. He looked at Vicaro. "Is there anything you would like to ask?"

"No, not right now," Vicaro replied.

"Fine," the doctor concluded. Within seconds, Dorothy was out of the trance and able to remember everything she had said.

She looked at Vicaro. "Where is that pool?"

"It's near the place where the two little kids were playing. I'll show you tomorrow."

"Dorothy, how do you feel?" asked Dr. Ribner.

"Never felt better. Got to find that little boy before my heart breaks."

"We will, and I think soon," Dr. Ribner predicted. "I would like to hypnotize you again next Saturday. Perhaps with time, we can desengage the little boy in your head. I don't know if he is stuck, or perhaps it is your own thoughts that are stuck. Only time will tell."

The following Saturday was agreed upon for the next session.

Tuesday evening Dorothy and her husband had dinner at Don Vicaro's house. Vicaro was anxious to have his wife meet Dorothy. Present at the meal was Mrs. Vicaro's sixteen-year-old brother, Robert, a tall, handsome boy wearing a high-school jacket.

Dorothy asked the boy if he liked motorcycles.

"Yes," he muttered.

Dorothy asked him if he knew anything about a "brand new red motorcycle with V-shaped ornamentation on its front?" She described the motorcycle in detail.

Robert said he had never seen one like it.

"Well, if you do," Dorothy warned, "be careful, because it could cause you injury."

"The next day," Vicaro later reported to Dorothy, "at a local ball park, Robert met an out-of-town friend who had just bought himself a new motorbike exactly like the one you described. The friend asked Robert to go for a ride."

Robert refused, telling his friend about the prediction. The friend laughed at such "nonsense" and took off on the new motorbike.

A few hundred yards down the road, a car shot out of a side street and struck the motorbike. The friend's arm was injured.

"Robert's face was white as a sheet when he came home and told us about the accident," Vicaro told Dorothy on the phone.

Dorothy was excited by Vicaro's news, because she felt she might have saved a boy's life.

A few days later Dorothy sat in her dining room working on her charts; astrological books and magazines, papers, and charts were spread out all over the dining-room table. She had already worked out the charts of Michael Kurscics and his parents, based on birth information the police had provided, to see if they supported her psychic vision.

Michael's parents were born into poor Polish families in New Jersey. Neither parent had a very stable astrological chart, especially when matched side by side. Dorothy wondered how a little five-year-old boy could be left in the care of his seven-year-old brother in such awful weather. The charts, however, helped her to understand the craziness that prevailed in the victim's home.

Looking at Lydia's chart, Dorothy discovered a point of what seemed to be personal tragedy in early childhood. Dorothy deduced that the incident had occurred when Lydia was in her tenth year. She looked into the mirror that covered the wall in her dining room and smiled. She felt she had made an important discovery, but she needed to meet Lydia to check it out.

Dorothy sat at the large table in her green flannel housecoat, two rollers in her hair, one over each ear. She felt that her life was only just beginning. Examining Lydia's chart—a woman considerably younger than herself, whose life looked difficult and whose prospects seemed not likely to improve—Dorothy felt compassion: compassion for the stranger whose child she somehow shared.

Dorothy lit a cigarette and went into the den, put her feet up on the couch, and looked at the photographs of her three children. They all shared her prominent brow and square jawline. She felt proud of her children. The world, she knew, could be terribly cruel. Children, no matter whose, needed protection. Her two sons had been raised with the ability to defend themselves, as had Justine, who could whip any boy on the block, if necessary.

The sound of the doorbell broke into her thoughts. Dorothy looked at the clock. It was already 10:30. She had worked on charts for two hours and had expected no visitors until lunchtime.

She buttoned her housecoat. The two rollers bounced in her hair as she went to the door. From the front window she caught a glimpse of Vicaro's patrol car.

"Dorothy." Vicaro moved into the house, out of the cold January day. "I'd like you to meet Lydia Kurscics."

Standing before Dorothy was a tall, thin woman wearing a long red coat, her hair pulled back under a brown knitted cap.

Dorothy took her hand, pumping it up and down. "I am so thankful to meet you. I was beginning to think Vic had personally hidden you."

The woman looked embarrassed. She assumed everyone knew that she had left her husband and children weeks before her son's disappearance. Now, standing before this psychic, Lydia Kurscics felt shy.

"Throw your coats on the couch," Dorothy instructed them. "Vic, put some water on the stove. I've got to run upstairs and put something on," she yelled as she darted up the staircase.

Moments later Dorothy stood before the kitchen sink, her back turned to her guests. "I've been extremely busy these last few weeks," she explained. "Please excuse the mess. My children keep me on the run. What's really keeping me busy," she turned to look at Lydia, "is your little boy. He just won't let go, and we can't find him. It's really too much for me."

Dorothy gently pushed coffee cups across the table and watched them skate, stopping just shy of their intended destinations. Each cup bore a different sign of the zodiac.

"Milk? Yeah, I can see you take milk," Dorothy said, reaching into the refrigerator.

Dorothy sat down at the table with her Capricorn cup and poured coffee all around. "Here, have a sweet roll, you're too thin." The box of rolls flew to Lydia's side.

Vicaro began. "I've told Lydia about your seeing Michael and how much time you've spent with us working on the case."

"I can't tell you how appreciative I am," Lydia said softly. "I'm afraid I have no money to repay you, but maybe my husband will be able . . ."

"Money?" Dorothy cut her short. "Who said anything about money? Vic isn't charging. Dr. Ribner didn't ask for anything. Saint Anthony never charged," she said, holding the medal around her neck. "I just want to find that poor little boy, that's all."

"Do you think you'll be able to find him?" Lydia asked. "You know they've already said the Mass of Angels for him."

"They didn't ask me about it. I would have told them to hold off," Dorothy said. "That's all right, now you know God is waiting for him and will protect him. Now that I've met you," she continued, "I know I will find him. Seeing you has confirmed for me the feeling that you are the mother of the boy I'm seeing. That's why I knew I had to meet you. Listen, Lydia, can I ask you something personal? Or should I kick Vicaro out first?" Dorothy asked.

Lydia turned red. "You can ask me anything in front of Vic, I guess," she stammered. She sat up stiffly and folded her arms before her.

Dorothy looked her in the eyes. "I see you were molested by your father when you were ten years old."

Vicaro turned white. Lydia gasped.

"I was nine," Lydia whispered, not sure if a correction was necessary.

Dorothy stamped her foot. "Sometimes I'm a year or two off, but I didn't know the exact time of birth," she said in her proud defense. Now Dorothy knew that she had a believer in Lydia Kurscics; she could tell the woman all about her son.

"I really feel for your kid, Lydia. That's why I've got to find him. We also have to do something with you," Dorothy said. "I know you have no place to go now. Right?" she probed.

Again Lydia was surprised. "You're right. I had an awful fight with the man I've been living with. I have no place to sleep and no job." Tears flowed down her cheeks.

"Well, just relax and we'll get some nourishment into those bones. You can stay right here until we find you a job. I've got plenty of room," Dorothy said spontaneously. "Woman need protection from men in the world," she said to Vicaro. "That's why there should be more women cops, so that women can be understood by the law, too."

Dorothy looked at the clock. It was 11:45 and she expected company for lunch. She placed a pile of small white onions on the Formica table, handed a knife to Lydia, and said, "Chop, sweetheart, we've got no more time to waste."

Lydia moved in that afternoon and shared a bedroom with Justine. It was not until the end of March, two months later, that she finally left the Allison house.

The following Saturday, January 23, Dr. Ribner warmly received Dorothy and Vic. Dorothy at once sat in the lounge chair. No long explanations were necessary. They all knew their roles. Dr. Ribner had already been briefed as to the previous week's progress.

"Doctor, I've been seeing lots of crazy things this week. I don't know why, but the world seems to be sleeping in my head." Dorothy dropped her head against the leather couch.

"We'll see what happens today," Dr. Ribner said as he adjusted the clamp to Dorothy's ear, regulated the dials, and lowered the shade.

"You're certainly looking well, Dorothy," the doctor said. "Maybe all those people rummaging around in there," he pointed to her head, "help keep you beautiful and thin."

"You know something," Dorothy smiled and looked at the doctor, "I think you're blind as a bat. Is this what psychiatrists do, tell funny-looking middle-aged women they're beautiful? Next time you'll probably tell me I look like Sophia Loren," she laughed.

Dr. Ribner blanched slightly at Dorothy's bluntness and decided he'd better get on with the questions. In moments he had her hypontized.

"Where do you see the boy?" he asked.

"He's not moving right now. He has been moving for awhile through the pipe. Yes, he has been flowing freely."

"Is he the only thing you see?" Dr. Ribner asked.

"No," Dorothy replied. "I see chunks of ice and little things, like garbage, moving around."

"Dorothy, do you think the boy is in the stream, or in a large river?" Ribner asked.

"Oh no, I'm sure it's not a river. I think he's in the sewer. But that's not where you're going to find him," Dorothy assured them.

"Where will we find him?" Vicaro asked.

"I've already described it to you. Where I saw him the first time. Wherever that is."

"Are you sure?" the officer pursued.

"Of course I'm sure," Dorothy sounded piqued.

"Why can't we find him there now?" Vicaro asked.

"Because he's not there now," Dorothy snapped. "You haven't even figured out where I'm talking about, to begin with."

Dr. Ribner felt Vicaro was pushing too hard, so he intervened.

"Dorothy," he said calmly, "relax for a second. Try to get a feeling of how long it will take Michael to get where you say we'll find him."

Dorothy's face was calm. Her entire body was limp as she searched for the moment the little boy would be discovered. The image of the little boy floating through the pipes faded in and out as other images blurred through. She remained quiet for a moment, trying to discern what was happening.

"Dorothy," Dr. Ribner called to her softly, "is something wrong? Are you seeing other things?"

"Yes, I don't know what, though. I've seen it before, recently. But now it's getting a little clearer." Her breathing quickened.

"What is it? Michael Kurscics?"

"No. Completely different," she said.

"What are you seeing?" The doctor moved closer to her.

"I see a kitchen. A huge kitchen with pots and pans all over the walls and huge counters. With a kitchen like that I could feed an army." She paused for a moment.

"I see a ship, too. A big ship like I saw coming into the city. There," she said, as if pointing to something all could witness. "I can't make out the letters on the ship. It's big black script. Not English, or anything like that. The letters are funny, like Greek letters.

"There's a dark man in the kitchen." Dorothy paused again. "Now there are a lot of people. People dressed up. Some of them have cameras. Pictures are flashing all around."

"Do you recognize any of them?" The doctor's voice was more excited.

"The faces aren't too clear. Wait a second," she held her breath. "I'm getting an image of someone." She strained for a clearer focus. "He looks familiar to me, but I can't see him clearly."

The room seemed consumed in a single breath, as Dorothy traveled through dimensions measureless to them in order to see. Both men sat transfixed.

"Who do you see?" Ribner gently probed.

"Kennedy," she said. Dorothy's voice was almost a whisper, as if she weren't positive of her vision. "I see one of the Kennedy boys. I don't know which one. Wait," she screamed. "Now I see two Kennedys."

"Which Kennedys?" Vicaro was anxious.

"*The* Kennedys!" Dorothy exclaimed. "What other Kennedys are there? I see both Robert and Teddy Kennedy. I think they're in trouble. At least, I feel that one of them is in serious trouble."

"Trouble? What kind of trouble?" the doctor asked.

"I'm not sure. I see a kitchen and a dark-skinned man. I feel he's the trouble. The dark man. If we find out who he is, then we'll know. But," she stopped for a second, "I think someone else in the kitchen might harm them, too."

"Know what?" Vicaro prodded.

"How should I know? I can't even tell which one is in real trouble."

"The ship, Dorothy, is it near the kitchen? Or is the kitchen on the ship?" the doctor pursued.

"No, they're two different places. I feel the ship is nearby. Here in New York. I see the writing is big on the side of the white ship."

Dr. Ribner considered the information for a moment, mentally scanning his familiarity with Mediterranean languages for one similar to Greek. He was Jewish and familiar with Hebrew script.

"Is the dark-skinned man connected with the boat?" he asked.

"I feel he is," Dorothy answered. "Maybe he came to this country on that ship. Maybe his parents did, I don't know."

"Does he work on the ship? Is he a crewman?"

"He's working for the United States, I feel."

Ribner looked at Vicaro. Both men looked surprised. Neither knew exactly what to do with the information. The doctor motioned to Vicaro, asking him if he had any further questions.

"Dorothy," Vicaro queried, "will Robert Kennedy be the next President of the United States?" President Johnson had just announced his decision not to run in the forthcoming election, and Robert Kennedy was a likely candidate.

Dorothy shook her head from side to side. Her eyes were closed, and she seemed anxious. She saw a newspaper headline, the word "Assassinated" across the top.

"No, no, he won't be President." Her breathing had quickened, her hands were holding tightly to the armrests. "I fear he'll be dead before then."

"Dorothy," Dr. Ribner intervened, "try and relax now. You're probably recalling President Kennedy's assassination. Let's try and focus on Michael Kurscics for a moment, then we'll talk about this later. Okay?" he said firmly, not wanting a response.

A minute later Dorothy reported she had the boy's face before her.

"Once again," Ribner led her, "try to sense how long it will take us to find Michael Kurscics."

"February seventh, around one-twenty in the afternoon," she said as if she had just checked her appointment book. "That's when we'll find him."

The two men were again excited, even stunned by her prediction.

"February seventh, around one twenty in the afternoon," Vicaro repeated aloud as he wrote it down in his notebook.

"That's right," Dorothy responded. "That's when someone will find Michael."

Vicaro looked at Ribner. "Now," he whispered, "if we only knew exactly where."

Dr. Ribner rose, lifted the shade, and looked out over the neighborhood buildings toward the west. "Okay, Dorothy, when I count to three, you will awaken and remember everything."

"Wait till I tell Justine I saw the Kennedys," Dorothy jumped out of the trance. "She won't believe it." She looked at Vicaro and the doctor. "Well, what are you thinking? I think we should get in a car and see if I can find that ship. What do you think?" Dorothy challenged them.

Both men looked at Dorothy. "I know what you're thinking, and you don't have to be psychic to see it. I'm not making this up. I see what I see," she shrieked. "I've got a house full of junk that needs to be cleaned. I don't have time either."

"Okay," Dr. Ribner moved toward his desk. "It's fine with me. I don't have an appointment until five, so we have plenty of time. Are you willing?" he asked Vicaro. "After all, it is your car."

"Sure," Vic snapped to his feet. "We've got to do something. I think I'll make a report of this, just in case."

Dorothy was in the waiting room already, wrestling with her new coat. "Report!" she exclaimed. "We've got to tell the FBI, or someone."

"I think we're a little premature, Dorothy. We should have at least one more session to see if we can get more information. You haven't exactly spelled out very much," Ribner suggested reasonably.

"We'll see," Dorothy replied from the elevator.

Two hours of driving up and down the West Side Highway produced no clear identification of a ship. Dorothy did recognize the script on a large freighter, though. The doctor thought it was Egyptian.

Vicaro's patience wore thin, so a date was made with the doctor for the following Saturday in Nutley, at Dorothy's home.

On Saturday Dorothy spent the whole morning feeding her family and straightening the house.

"There's a very important doctor coming here with Officer Vicaro, so I don't want to hear your voices anywhere. You can go over to a friend's house and stay all afternoon," Dorothy told Justine and Paul.

The prospect of finding the little boy excited Dorothy. By the time Ribner and Vicaro arrived, she had worked

68

herself into a frenzy. Boxes of pastries and piles of canned goods were being hurled into their proper quarters when Dorothy heard the doorbell. She had successfully booted everyone out of the house. She went to the door with hands full.

"Dorothy, we've interrupted you," the polite doctor took her hand.

"No, no, come on in. I've been expecting you. I just never seem to get my work finished. My children always seem to be needing more and more, instead of less and less."

The two men entered the house, and Dorothy gave the door a light kick with her foot. Ribner saw the baby grand piano and ran his fingers over the keys.

"One of my sons plays beautifully," she told them. "One day he'll study at Julliard."

"Dorothy," Vicaro interrupted, "do I hear whistling somewhere?"

"Oh, it's the water boiling," she said, and disappeared into the kitchen. She called to them from the stove. "Come on in here. You've got to have a little nourishment first."

The two men proceeded into the kitchen. Dr. Ribner noticed a painting on the wall of John F. Kennedy walking in a celestial field in shirt-sleeves. Next he noticed the astrological calendar on the wall. "What does today look like?" he asked her.

"Well, my chart is not very good today. There are definitely signs for caution in my chart," she warned them.

"I know you are a Leo," she said to Ribner. "It's not the day for you to make a total discovery, either."

He smiled. "I suppose you're right. There's a lot of illness in my family right now."

"We won't find the kid today, but we'll get closer. You two finish this and we can go to work," Dorothy poured more coffee.

As the second cup was downed, Dr. Ribner explained the virtues of using sodium amatyl, or truth serum. Vicaro had suggested the use of the drug. Dorothy felt a new jolt of anxiety at the prospect of being injected with anything, especially truth serum.

"This way," Dr. Ribner explained, "I can control the

level of hypnosis more closely. If you're being blocked, perhaps we can break through."

"Break through my brain, that's what you'll do. Well," she sighed, "here I go again."

Dr. Ribner erected the IV stand in Dorothy's bedroom, and her right arm was bared for the injection. She lay on her bed, nervous and squeamish at the sight of the medical equipment. Now she felt terribly alone in her own home. She had sent her family away, and now she longed to hear their footsteps.

"Count slowly backward from a hundred," Dr. Ribner said, pressing the needle into her arm and regulating the drip-by-drip movement through the clear tube. Dorothy's mind seemed to soften, the outer world easing away as she relaxed.

"Dorothy, how are you?" Dr. Ribner began the inquiry.

"I feel okay. A little heavy around the eyes, but I'm okay."

"Good. Now, let's concentrate on Michael Kurscics. Do you remember where you saw him last?"

"Yes. But I don't think he's there now. I see his little body, and it's not moving. Last time he was moving."

"What about above him?" Dr. Ribner asked.

"I see the ITT, the school, and a hill. I think there are three pieces of lumber on that hill. It's a pretty steep incline."

Vicaro remembered the details as being similar to Dorothy's original dream. For the first time she seemed to be returning to the site she described almost two months prior. Vicaro was hopeful.

"Is there any sort of hardware store in the area?" the patrolman pursued.

Dorothy thought for a moment, as her inner eye telescoped the area in search of details, symbols that would identify the location.

"Yes," she said calmly. "I see a lumberyard above the hill."

"Can you see the ITT building from the hill?"

"Yes, but it's further away from Michael Kurscics."

As she said his name, her body began to tighten and contract. Dr. Ribner and Vicaro watched her reacting to

70

some inner vision, not knowing what to do. Dr. Ribner let another drop of liquid enter Dorothy's vein, in the hope of calming her.

Her body relaxed for a moment. Drops of perspiration speckled her forehead. She was warm and felt nauseated.

Michael Kurscics's eyes opened before her, as if he were looking straight at hers. Eye to eye, Dorothy felt her stomach ache, her neck muscles tense, and her jaw clamp down.

"The eyes. I see his eyes and they're haunting. I feel like he's trying to tell me something. What a pitiful sight. I feel him. I see him. He's stuck. How he wants to move. He needs to move. Oh, my stomach," she gasped, bending in half.

Worlds of strength and psychic power combined in Dorothy's being as her body reacted both to the emerging child and to the drug.

She felt her head spinning, distancing her from the other world where the two men stood in suspense, not knowing what was happening. She was at once the seer, the mover, the little boy, the dead body. She was both the inertia and the movement.

Dorothy's flesh was hot and perspiring. A fear pervaded her consciousness that she would not have the strength to move the little boy. As she merged with the universe and the little boy, she felt a rush of waters and energy overtake her, the flow of which carried Michael Kurscics nearer to his final resting-place. Dorothy knew her entire being had given way to the child, that every part of her body, physically and spiritually, was drained. She felt a sudden burst of fluid as though she was giving birth.

In her delirium she whispered to the two men, "He's free now. He's moving toward the place he'll be found. Oh, God, help me. What has happened to me?" and she slipped from consciousness.

The doctor checked her pulse and breathing. She was excited, but everything seemed normal. He looked at her face. She looked like a mother who had just given birth.

Hours passed before Dorothy regained consciousness. Her body ached; her head rang with the pressure of her clamped jaws. The sheets were tossed about her, damp with perspiration. They were also stained. She had her period.

She managed to get up and bathe, and the warm water soothed her body.

Over and beyond her physical discomfort Dorothy was depressed and frightened. The drugs gave her a shrouded feeling, as if a pall were over her. She had no strength to fight.

The next day Vicaro suggested they might make another stab at driving around.

"If he's free, then maybe we'll find him."

"Vicaro," Dorothy explained, "I am what is known as tired. My body feels like a used car that was hit by a crane. And," she added, "I look like one, too.

"Please, I said Michael would not be found until February seventh. There is no sense in trying to outguess what is destined. Nine times out of ten, fate wins."

"Okay, Dorothy. Have it your way. If I get a chance, I'll look myself. How's Lydia?"

"She needs a job."

"I'll ask around," Vicaro offered.

Dorothy did not regret having taken in Lydia. Growing up without money or resources, she had known many down-and-out people. Moreover she felt that women had it hardest in society, and Lydia impressed her as a woman who had suffered in a man's world. It was almost time, she felt, that Michael was found and his mother sent on her way.

Thinking about February 7, Dorothy could not explain why she felt so strongly about the date. Astrologically the day was a good one not only in her chart, but in the victim's as well. But that didn't fully explain the feeling she had about that day. She, like everyone else, would have to wait and see.

She reflected over the past month and the changes that had occurred in her life. Powers and abilities she had never known in herself had somehow chosen this time in her life to come out, giving her a sense of rebirth.

As she grew more accustomed to living and dealing with her psyche, Dorothy would develop abilities that allowed her to gain more and more control and focus. Now she knew that believing in herself was the most important thing.

The biggest news in the New York area on February 5 was the weather; for on that day the temperature inexplicably began to rise. For three days the sun radiated springlike heat in the dead of winter. The temperature reached a high of sixty degrees.

At noon on February 7 Bill Werner left work to return home in Clifton, New Jersey, to eat his lunch. His wife, Sylvia, had called him at work that morning to tell him that Mamie, their cat, was dead. "What am I supposed to do with a dead cat?" his wife cried.

Bill agreed to return at lunch and take care of the dead animal. He decided that after two days of warm weather the soil would be in good enough condition for digging a small hole. He would take the cat over to the nearby water hole, Bleachery Pond, and bury it there.

When he arrived at home, his wife told him the trying saga she had suffered, discovering Mamie in the clothes hamper, dead.

"How could I lift her up?" she said. "It's so awful."

As he walked to the bathroom and contemplated the sight he would probably encounter, his stomach turned. Nausea would overcome him if he allowed it to.

Bill placed the stiff black cat into a burlap bag and placed it in his trunk. He drove to the side of the elementary school, just above Bleachery Pond. He looked out and saw the ITT tower standing tall in Nutley and the Shell station on the highway, above the pond.

With sack in hand he began the steep descent to the water's edge. The ground was still moist from the snows. Barren branches caught in his coat. Several times he had to retrace his steps where the underbrush was impassable.

His eyes searched the water's edge for a possible resting-place for Mamie. Suddenly Bill Werner stopped short and put Mamie down. His eyes, he hoped, deceived him.

He edged closer to the water, careful not to trip. There, approximately seven feet in front of him, floated the remains of Michael Kurscics.

73

It was 1:30 when Bill Werner called the Clifton Police Department to inform them of his discovery. Twenty minutes later a call was placed to the neighboring Nutley Police Department for a missing-person's check.

Vicaro had been sent out to check on an accident in the Shop Rite parking lot just prior to the Clifton call. When he got back to the department around three, the sergeant told him that the Kurscics kid had been found.

Vicaro bounded up the steps to Buel's office.

"I hear they found the kid," he said to the chief.

Buel told him that the boy's body was found floating along the edge of the Bleachery Pond in Clifton, across the highway.

Vic called Dorothy and told her to prepare Lydia; he was coming to pick them up and take them to the funeral home for identification. He told her not to tell Lydia that the boy had been found, because he wanted to hypnotize her first, helping her to prepare psychologically for what she was going to see.

Vicaro did hypnotize the mother and prepare her. As it turned out, however, she never identified her son. Vicaro did, and later the father.

The funeral director asked Dorothy, "Are these the clothes you saw in your vision?" He showed her a plastic bag containing the child's snowsuit. She blanched; her insides quivered as she identified the clothing as that seen in her vision.

Not only was Dorothy correct about the date of Michael's recovery, but everything he wore was exactly as she had seen. It was the funeral director who mentioned the boy's overshoes were on the wrong feet. And his hands, which Dorothy had seen as charred, were dark with mud.

Dorothy prayed to St. Anthony, thanking him for his assistance in helping her. The burial of the little boy was paid for by Dorothy, as the parents could not afford it.

Chapter 4

Finding Michael Kurscics changed Dorothy's life forever.
Never again could she deny the import of her visions, nor
the fear she was experiencing. At the age of forty-three
Dorothy had spent most of her life raising her family. But
the little drowning victim had become a part of her soul,
as would dozens of other children in the coming years.
Little Michael's face would never leave Dorothy's mind,
sometimes bringing her comfort, sometimes sadness.

Dorothy now began to see more and more, but she still
understood very little. Images of death or unknown faces
would creep into her consciousness without warning or
emotional preparation. For the next several years the
usually buoyant woman would often teeter between emotions, many times forcing her to retreat into solitude. Concerned for her welfare, her husband and children imposed
a moratorium on her work.

Word eventually got around to neighboring police departments of her success with Michael Kurscics. They
would call on Dorothy to help them on dead-end cases.
From Newark to the northern reaches of New Jersey, police came to her with robberies, assault and batteries, missing persons, and arson cases.

Though she sometimes would try and help the police,

her abilities were mostly in the abstract. She had not yet learned to focus and interpret images that came to her, though she was willing to try. Nor did she have anyone, except Vicaro and Justine, who would sit down and listen to her visions. Often Dorothy and Justine would talk about the people she saw, the mother hoping to find in her daughter both an identifier and a sympathetic ear: Justine was both.

Justine and Paul loved to hear of their mother's involvements with the police, often coming home to find a patrol car sitting in front of their house. But they were also frightened when they saw their ebullient mother plunged into depression by an inexplicable vision. Dorothy would try not to reveal the horrors she saw to her family, but they could see how she was affected. Bob and Justine would take over the cooking and shopping when they felt she needed total rest.

The summer after Dorothy found Michael Kurscics she received a call from an acquaintance who reported the son of her closest friend missing. Eighteen-year-old Barney Berke had gone to Asbury Park on a date with his girl friend, Molly. Barney and Molly had been spending the day on the beach when Barney said he wanted to fetch something from his car, and he left, supposedly to return momentarily. But he never came back. Barney had disappeared, wearing only a bathing suit, and with his car still parked where he had left it.

The Berkes were frantic. The area was scoured by police and detectives for days, but Barney was not found. Daily the parents went to the shore and watched over the ocean for any sign of their son. Helicopters and boats provided no more clues.

Dorothy listened to the voice of the mother on the phone, which helped her form a picture of the son. She immediately felt that the boy was not dead, though she saw that he was trapped in some entanglement.

"I don't see him drowned or dead at all," Dorothy told the parents. "I know he will return. He's caught in some kind of Houdini act. You will just have to be patient. He will return."

Two months passed and the Berkes lost patience. The mother told Dorothy she didn't want to hear her predictions anymore because they only gave her and her husband false hopes. She informed Dorothy that they were planning a funeral for their son.

The night before the funeral Dorothy called the parents to say that she felt they were wrong in losing faith, but that she had done everything she could to help.

Two weeks after the funeral Barney Berke reappeared at his home, bedraggled and wearing ill-fitting clothes. He told his parents he had been a victim of amnesia, and had no recollection of his whereabouts for the past months, nor could he remember who had given him his attire.

The "Houdini act" Dorothy had seen was later explained by the apologetic parents. Barney was studying to be a professional magician, and the psychic had obviously picked up this aspect of his life.

Regardless of occasional successes, Dorothy was still too emotionally involved with her visions to be able to objectify and interpret. Sleepless nights of agonizing dreams rendered her vulnerable and without resistance.

As the years went on, she would take on occasional cases. In 1973, she was asked by New York's *Midday Live* television show to appear with writer William Blatty, whose new book, *The Exorcist*, had just been published.

One of the program's viewers was a detective from the New Brunswick Police Department. Phyllis Thompson, a twenty-eight-year-old schoolmaster, had been brutally murdered on September 2, 1973, in East Brunswick, New Jersey. In one of Dorothy's finest psychic sleuthings since the Michael Kurscics case, she was able to describe with alarming detail the victim's last hour, giving not only the birth dates of the last two people to see her, but the murderer's name and background, as well.

A detective from the East Brunswick police called the Nutley Police Department in search of Dorothy. On Dorothy's first visit to East Brunswick with the detective, she led them directly to the bar where Phyllis had been having a nightcap with friends.

The mother later detailed the events in the following manner:

Mrs. Allison told me she saw Phyllis being forced into a car, raped, struck three times with a heavy object, and drowned. All of these things were indeed found to be true. She further described a cemetery where the man took the body. It was the very cemetery the body was actually taken to.

Mrs. Allison said the murderer's name was Krug. She gave his birthday and said he was short with powerful arms. He was an ex-convict. He had even hurt his leg the last time he was in jail. The police found all of this was indeed the case when Krug was arraigned.

She mentioned that Phyllis's wristwatch would show the time 3:25 A.M. When the body was found, the watch had stopped at that very time.

One of her most important clues, which she mentioned on the very first visit, concerned an article of Phyllis's clothing. She said Krug tried to burn the clothes, but that a fingerprint of Krug's would remain on Phyllis's panty hose. This was found and used later as a major piece of evidence in the trial. She said Krug would be picked up while committing another crime. Her description exactly fit that of Frederick Krug, twenty-seven, of South River, New Jersey. He had just been picked up on alleged charges of rape and had a long record of violent attacks on young women.

Thanks to Mrs. Allison, Krug was indicted for the murder of Phyllis Thompson on January 16, 1974. He was sentenced to life imprisonment for the kidnap-murder.

Although saddened and often sickened by the sight of the victims, whether child or adult, Dorothy believed that finding a body and therefore being able to have a funeral were as comforting as anything else that might be done. She came to feel that a funeral at least put an end to the torture, and as a concluding rite, helped some faltering families begin to reestablish a more normal pattern, and sometimes brought them closer to God again. In the period between the Michael Kurscics case and her work on the Phyllis Thompson murder, she gradually learned to render her own sadness into positive energy and focus on her objectives: finding the victim and then, if possible, the culprit.

Waiting, in Dorothy's mind, was torture. Part of her mission in her new life, she hoped, would be to end the interminable period of waiting, speculation, and false hope for the parents of missing children. She saw firsthand how parents were destroyed by the lack of resolve, never knowing if their child ran away for emotional reasons, or was abducted. As long as there remained a chance that word would come of the missing child, parents always kept the fire of hope alive. Dorothy felt, particularly if she saw the victim dead, that hope was another ingredient in the torture.

One of Dorothy's greatest gifts, which would help endear her to the staunchest police skeptic, was her comic aspect. The child in Dorothy was an important source of life. From that irrepressible side of herself she would summon the spirit of adventure and faith, of humor and unadulterated compassion for others. Laughter, she felt, was the antidote to tragedy and her greatest defense against overwhelming depression. The child in her loved to play pranks, often using her psychic powers as the source of humor. The fact that most of the police she would deal with towered over her in height and bulk made her antics seem all the more childlike.

The blossoming of her psychic abilities opened up channels of her intellect she had never before realized she possessed. Her ability to objectify herself and call to account her various personal aspects would allow her to question the prejudices with which she had grown up. Through the years Dorothy would become a campaigner on issues she learned about from her new encounters with people from all backgrounds. And while a firm believer in God, she could be both iconoclastic and irreverent.

* * *

On February 8, 1974, Dorothy was asked by Randolph Hearst to assist him in finding his daughter, Patty, who had been kidnapped on February 4. Dorothy, before that weekend, had never heard of either Randolph or Patty Hearst.

"Would you help us? We're desperate," Hearst pleaded with Dorothy. He would fly her out and pay whatever price she requested for her services.

"I don't take money, Mr. Hearst. There's no price for a child."

During that weekend Dorothy had watched coverage of the kidnapping on television. All she knew was that a teenage girl had been taken and the girl's parents had money. Dorothy agreed to fly to San Francisco and work under hypnosis for two days. She would bring two people with her, she told Hearst, so she would need fare and rooms for three: Dorothy, Vicaro, and Dr. Ribner, her psychic guide and interrogator. Carmen A. Orechio, Director of Public Safety for the town of Nutley, cooperated by allowing Detective Vicaro to accompany Dorothy.

Hearst agreed, and the trio flew to California. For two days Ribner and Vicaro worked with Dorothy and the FBI, going over clues and details of Patty's life that might trigger something in Dorothy's psyche. Dorothy spent hours under hypnotic trance, being interrogated about places and people she had never heard of or seen.

They worked while hundreds of agents, detectives, and police across the country built a network of communication in the most publicized kidnapping the world had witnessed since the Lindbergh child had been reported missing.

In her hotel room perched over the bay, Dorothy searched for Patty. She could do little more than say the girl was still alive, frightened, and hidden in a place that was dark, like a prison cell. "There is a small light in the room," she explained. "It's dark like a closet."

Time and again she saw the girl alive in a dark cell. She could describe the room with some accuracy of detail, but she could not determine its whereabouts.

Dorothy left San Francisco to work on other cases, telling Hearst and the FBI that she would work on his daughter's case from her home. But it was not until five months later that she had a psychic run-in with Patty Hearst while searching for the bodies of two men in central Pennsylvania.

On July 20, Dorothy had been in Hollidaysburg, Pennsylvania, looking for the bodies of Richard Wyler and Alfred Sutley, New Jersey and Long Island businessmen whose single-engine Beechcraft had plunged into the night somewhere between Cincinnati and Teterboro, New Jersey, on July 10.

Ruth Wyler, wife of forty-nine-year-old victim, had contacted Dorothy from her Westwood, New Jersey, home. She explained to Dorothy that the last time the men had been heard from was from the Flight Service Station at Johnstown, Pennsylvania, not far from Altoona, at 8:00 P.M. on July 10.

Despite the combined efforts of the Federal Aviation Administration and local and state police, as well as a five-state search by the Civil Air Patrol, the plane had not been found, Mrs. Wyler reported.

Mrs. Wyler later gave the following statement to Dorothy:

Mrs. Allison worked by providing description, of people, places, and things, that she felt were relevant to the case. To further aid us, she went through three hours of detailed questioning under hypnosis which was taped for later reference. It is necessary to interpret her material and for this she collaborated with the Civil Air Patrol units, the state police, and knowledgeable local citizens. She also spent ten days hiking in the mountains working with these groups, our two sons, and me. Early in July she predicted that if the plane was not found by July 15, it would be found on December 9, as it was.

The affidavit goes on to say that "the plane made a U-turn" in Dorothy's description, and when found, the plane was heading west, not east, as it should have been heading; she reported the plane "leaving a trail, and the tail of the plane separated from the plane," whereas it had indeed crashed through the trees, leaving a trail of plane parts and belongings over a 350-yard path. Dorothy saw "cotton candy all over the ground," and the night it crashed the weather reports indicated the site was shrouded in fog.

"I see checkered jackets," Dorothy had reported.

Both men were wearing checkered jackets.

"The men aren't together," she said.

Only one man was found in the plane, the other having been blown some twenty feet away by the impact.

During one of the early hypnosis sessions Dorothy was told to get in a car and drive toward the wreck from New York City. Mrs. Wyler reports that "through questioning we led her through New Jersey en route to Pennsylvania, where we were convinced the plane had gone down. Mrs. Allison strongly objected to leaving New Jersey. Had we allowed her to follow her own instincts and questioned her more skillfully as to her reasons for wanting to stay in New Jersey, perhaps we could have found the plane earlier."

While in central Pennsylvania Dorothy had gotten some feelings about Patty Hearst. She felt Patty was somewhere in the area, somewhere in Pennsylvania. She insisted upon calling the FBI agent in San Francisco who was in charge of the Hearst case. From the state police office in Hollidaysburg Dorothy reported to the agent that Patty was in Pennsylvania in a farmhouse, not in California as they felt. He accepted the information and gave her the name of an agent in Johnstown whom she could call if she got anything more specific. She did contact the Johnstown agent, calling him at home at 2:00 A.M., reporting to the sleeping agent that she was a psychic and that she felt strongly about Patty Hearst being in the area.

"What?" the dubious agent asked. "You saw Patty Hearst in Hollidaysburg?"

"No, I didn't say I did. I said I feel she is in Pennsylvania, not California. I see her in my head," Dorothy explained.

"Are you for real lady? How did you get my number?" His voice did not hide his agitation.

Dorothy gave him the name of the agent in San Francisco. "He said to call you if I felt anything about Patty being in the area," Dorothy said, not pleased at the credibility problem.

"You live in Hollidaysburg?" the agent asked.

"No, I don't live here. I'm looking for two bodies and a missing airplane. I live in New Jersey."

The thoroughly confused agent said he would check with headquarters the next morning. He quickly said good-bye and hung up.

Months later it was discovered that Patty Hearst *had* been in Pennsylvania at the time of Dorothy's call. However Dorothy had no way of knowing whether the agent she had spoken to had ever acted on her call.

On December 9, Ruth Wyler called Dorothy to say that the remains of the airplane and the two men had been found not in Pennsylvania, but in Morris County, New Jersey, in an area very much like that described by Dorothy during hypnosis. A hunter trekking through the woods half a mile south of Jefferson Township Middle School had found the plane's wreckage unburned, as Dorothy had envisioned.

Ruth Wyler expressed her thanks and allegiance to Dorothy and her work.

"You've put my mind at ease," Dorothy told Mrs. Wyler. "Not bad marksmanship, finding the plane on the day I predicted. My stars are in a good place today."

Dorothy felt terrific that week as she prepared for the holidays. Articles appeared in the papers from Altoona to Nutley claiming that Dorothy's predictions had been corroborated five months after the plane had crashed.

The next day Dorothy was pleased to find a letter from Catherine Hearst thanking her for the St. Anthony statue the psychic had sent as a gift. She thanked her, as well, for the efforts she had made in the investigation. The mother of the still-missing girl expressed her faith in God and the hope that Patty would be found alive, as Dorothy insisted. Dorothy continued to work on the Hearst case with New York FBI Agent Bob McDowell.

On Friday, December 13, Dorothy took Justine and Paul for an early dinner and some shopping at the neighboring Bloomfield shopping center. Thousands of pre-Christmas shoppers prowled through the stores, bumping into one another with the resignation of the inevitable.

While Dorothy and her children pranced around the mall, fate prepared to alter the life of another shopper that evening.

Francis Carlucci, a heavyset, quiet, unassuming mother of four from Colonia, New Jersey, was shopping with her daughters Justine and Doreen, and Doreen's new girl friend, Joanne Delardo. Francis moved slowly and patiently after a long day of work as a nurse at Rahway Hospital, thinking about the presents she had yet to buy for her children, husband, and parents.

Joe Carlucci, her husband, had taken their two sons for haircuts, and would retrieve the women at an appointed spot. Joe Carlucci, a machinist for fifteen years, had worked closely with his wife to raise a family who believed in God and the freedoms that their country offered. Religion formed a strong foundation for the Carlucci family: that foundation's strength would soon be tested.

The night was clear and crisp. Everyone's mind was on gifts and holiday spirits and the tree that was to be picked out on Sunday.

When the family arrived back at their split-level home, Doreen, fourteen years old, and her friend Joanne, fifteen, discussed evening plans while the rest of the family unpacked purchases and talked about the exciting things they had seen in the stores.

Doreen stood at the kitchen phone, leaning on the Formica counter, checking with friends about the evening's recreation, mindlessly doodling on a note pad a cartoon of shoes and feet. Of medium height and attractively slim, Doreen was feeling particularly good because she had just had her long, dark hair cut into a more modern short style, like her girl friends'. She wanted to show it off that night.

Bright, compassionate, and artistic, Doreen had a niche in her heart for the underdog; she had befriended one or two boyfriends whom others felt were undesirable. A student at Colonia Junior High, her grades were very good and her participation in school activities enthusiastic.

She had become friends with Joanne, who lived several

84

blocks away and was a year ahead of her in school, through Joanne's sixteen-year-old brother, Joseph. A junior in high school, Joseph liked Doreen and had visited the Carlucci house on several occasions. Friday, December 13, was the first time Joanne had ever visited the Carlucci house, and was the last time Francis and Joe saw either girl alive.

The girls decided to go to the Delardo house to watch a Christmas special on the Delardos' color television. Francis called Jeannette Delardo, whom she had never met, to see if it was okay with her.

"No problem," Mrs. Delardo said. "I'll be home all evening. Doreen's welcome here."

Francis told Doreen that 11:00 P.M. was the latest she could be out. She kissed her daughter on the forehead and went back to wrapping presents.

Doreen and Joanne watched the television special and then walked the eight blocks to St. John Vianney Church where a coffeehouse called Shalom House was sponsored on weekends to give the teen-agers a place to get together.

At 11:15, Francis called the Delardos to find out whether Doreen had left for home yet. She found that her daughter had gone to the Shalom House, and the girls were expected home momentarily. At 11:45, Francis got into her car and drove to the church, where teen-agers were talking in the parking lot.

Two friends of Doreen's reported that they had last seen the two girls sitting on the steps, eating ice cream. That was at around 10:00 P.M. No one had seen them since. No one knew where they were heading, or if they had any plans.

At 4:00 A.M., Francis and Joe phoned the Woodbridge Police Department to report their missing child. Francis, normally a quiet worrier, had to stop several times during the policeman's questioning to stifle the rush of tears. The police reported they had not heard of any problems in the area.

On Friday, December 20, Detective Salvatore Lubertazzi sat in the Nutley Police Department thinking that the clock was crawling at a snail's pace. "What could be accomplished in the next hour," he wondered, "before splitting for home?"

Christmas always had its freak emergencies; incidents of vandalism and theft also ran higher than at other times of the year. The holiday season always brought out the difficulties in life, with Santas on every corner as reminders of loneliness and economic strife. The detective smiled, recalling a Santa they had picked up for pickpocketing people who were standing on the corner waiting for the light to change. He had turned out to be a bald former Hare Krishna follower.

A call did come that Lubertazzi, known as Lupo, had to handle: a call that would lead the shy Italian down on a trail of frustration, sadness, and discovery.

The call came from Nutley resident Elaine DeMars, who lived with her husband, John, and their two little boys in a quiet, well-to-do neighborhood. The woman's voice was nervous but contained. She had never had occasion to call the police before.

Lupo listened while the woman explained that her husband, an upstanding citizen, a man of reliability, an officer of the Chemical Bank of New York, was missing.

"He calls if he's going to be five minutes late," the twenty-six-year-old wife said. "It doesn't stand to reason that he would stay out late at a friend's without letting me know."

Six feet three inches tall, weighing over two hundred pounds, John DeMars lived his life with regularity and reason. A man of habit, he parked his car each morning at the Delawanna Station in Nutley, rode the Erie Lackawanna Railway to Hoboken, where he picked up the PATH train to the Church Street stop, four blocks from his Chemical Bank branch. The same route, in reverse, was repeated each evening, getting him home between 6:30 and 7:00 P.M.

With only half of their Christmas shopping done, and tree ornaments still sitting in the box ready to adorn the tree, Elaine DeMars sat anxiously as the minutes and hours passed and still no word from her husband came.

By 10:00 she had called every possible friend or bank acquaintance, looking for her husband. Two friends who had lunched with him said he had talked about bowling that night. She also found out from his secretary that he had left the office full of holiday spirit, saying he was looking forward to playing with his kids over the weekend. That was the last time anyone reported having talked to him.

Lupo went to the DeMars home where he took down the information from Elaine DeMars and John DeMar's mother and brother-in-law, a deacon in the diocese of Paterson, New Jersey. When they had finished talking, Lupo thought to himself that the description of the missing man given by the family made him think a saint was missing, not a mortal.

John DeMars was an unlikely candidate for the many possible explanations the detectives had to pursue: a 1966 Rutgers graduate, a former intelligence officer in Vietnam, assistant manager of commercial accounts at Chemical Bank, a district deputy of the Knights of Columbus and a past Grand Knight of Council 6159, plus the father of two boys. A man like John DeMars would be difficult to lose between the cracks.

Investigatory agencies, like all bureaucracies, observe weekends and holidays to some degree. If a person is reported missing on Friday, the wheels of the investigation do not begin to turn until Monday. It is also standard procedure to wait twenty-four hours before full-scale investigation begins on a case; in many instances a missing person shows up, having forgotten to mention a prior engagement or having been lost in someone's arms.

Beginning Monday morning, Deputy Chief Salvatore Dimichino coordinated the efforts of his men, the newspaper, television, and radio stations. Chief Buel put the investigation in his charge, asking for a daily report on his findings. Each evening Dimichino would sit with Lupo, analyzing the steps that had been covered that day, taking in the phone calls of people reporting having seen the man whose photo appeared in newspapers throughout the New Jersey and New York metropolitan area.

After five days of investigation they had come up with nothing more than the clockwork routine of a man who seldom, if ever, was deflected from his daily course. Dimi-

87

chino was baffled as he heard about the hundreds of interviews his men conducted in Nutley, in the subway stations, on the train platform, and the train itself, without a single clue to the man's whereabouts.

A missing person stops time and alters life irrevocably for the family. Suddenly a phone ringing becomes a symbol, one that Francis Carlucci, Jeannette Delardo, and Elaine DeMars listened for constantly in tearful hope that the next call would be the familiar voice that resounded in their dreams, in their prayers, in their every waking moment. Waiting for the unknown to be disclosed is torture to thousands each year whose family members are reported missing.

Each evening Lupo sat with the DeMars family and gave them a progress report. Passengers on the train were being questioned, he told them, as well as cabdrivers. Some commuters recognized the photograph of DeMars, having silently traveled with him to and from Manhattan, briefly acknowledging one another over newspapers and briefcases. The conductor and train personnel had also been questioned and all recognized DeMars, but no one confirmed his having been on the train that evening.

"If Mr. DeMars left 199 Church Street at four-thirty P.M., then he would have been at the World Trade Center subway station in time to catch the five-oh-five PATH train for Hoboken," Lupo explained. "But there was a delay in the PATH that night, so he had to take a later train, and would have been on the five-twenty Erie Lackawanna."

A PATH official confirmed that there had been a ten-minute delay in service on that line during the December 20 rush hour because of equipment problems.

Possibilities of kidnapping were investigated thoroughly, since any bank official has access to material and information that might provoke a crime. Bank records and notes afforded no explanations for the police, as well DeMars' files were in perfect order and no money had been removed from his own account apart from the usual weekend fare.

Lupo's heart weighed heavily each time he left the DeMars home. A Christmas tree sat in their living room, unlit and simply decorated; no presents were visible. Expecting her husband to walk in at any time, Elaine DeMars had decided to leave the tree ready for celebration.

Each evening Lupo went home to his wife, Phyllis, and their five children. A detective with a great store of compassion and an unprepossessing manner, Lupo spent much of his time wondering how so much suffering existed in the world.

As a child growing up in Nutley, he had experienced anti-Italian feelings that lingered still in his reticent, if not shy, demeanor. Underneath his facade remained a hard core of skepticism, however, that would soon be tested by Dorothy.

The day before Christmas, at 8:30 that chilly morning, Dorothy received a call from Francis Carlucci. The hushed-voiced woman from Colonia explained that one of Dorothy's neighbors, whom Dorothy had never met, was an old school chum of hers and had reported to her that Dorothy had psychic abilities. The tearful caller wondered whether Dorothy might have a moment to spend with her as her daughter had been missing with her fifteen-year-old-old girl friend since Friday, December 13.

"She had no reason to run away." Francis's tone was adamant after weeks of listening to police theorize and insist that her daughter had, indeed, run away. She had pointed out that the girl's $50.00 in Christmas money still sat on her dresser.

Dorothy believed the mother. She could feel instantly that the girls had not run away. She could not tell if they were still living, but her inclination weighed heavily toward the belief that they were dead.

"Could we come up and see you, Mrs. Allison?" Francis Carlucci asked. "Whenever is good for you."

"Would you wait till Thursday so I can spend Christmas with my family? I'm having twenty-seven people for dinner tomorrow. Anyway, you should spend tomorrow thanking God you have other beautiful children," Dorothy advised.

Francis didn't know what to say. Had she mentioned her other children to the psychic?

"Also," Dorothy said, "bring one or two articles belonging to the girls. You know, a necklace or a glove, or better yet, something they loved wearing. And bring the exact time of birth for both girls. Be sure it's the exact moment. That's very important," the psychic instructed.

Francis thanked Dorothy and told her that her prayers would include her. A Roman Catholic, Francis's faith in God was being tested beyond any of her prior experiences. A woman who spent her days caring for the sick and her evenings tending and loving her family was a sadly ironic candidate for the tragedy she and her family were suffering.

In her mind Francis connected Dorothy with her faith in God. She felt certain that Dorothy's spiritual and psychic abilities were closely knitted to her own faith. Before she ever met the Nutley psychic, she believed in her, as she believed in God.

Early Thursday afternoon Bob Allison opened the door for the Carluccis, the Delardos and the Carluccis' Nutley friend, Maureen. They all sat down in the Allisons' den, where Dorothy served food and introduced Justine and Paul to the families, telling them that she felt certain she would find their children within the next three days.

Any trepidation the strangers might have been feeling was quickly assuaged by the familial spirit of Dorothy's home. Justine and Paul told them about other cases Dorothy had worked on, and resolved, most of them within thirty days.

The doorbell rang again, and Dorothy shouted that the door was unlocked and that Jason was in the basement. The door opened, revealing the energetic and smiling face of Don Vicaro. Dorothy kissed him and wished him a happy holiday. Then she introduced him to the two Colonia families.

"This man has worked with me on cases over the last several years and can help interpret things that I'm seeing," Dorothy explained. "Let's sit in the living room and talk seriously."

The parents of the missing girls told the story of the night their daughters disappeared, and the police investigation that ensued. In solemn detail the families told how a thirteen-state alarm was in effect; of the days and nights that schoolmates, relatives, neighbors, and rescue-squad volunteers had joined in an intensive search in the towns of Colonia, Edison, Clark, and Rahway; of questioning dozens of schoolmates and subjecting them to polygraphs; of walking through dense brush and forests in the cold rain and snow; of finding caves and holes and hoping against hope that their children might be buried there; of the dozens of crank calls and hopeful sightings of their little girls; of the $1,500 reward that was offered; of posting the girls' photographs on bulletin boards in shopping centers, office buildings, schools, and shop windows; and of the desperation and futility they had faced.

While they spoke, Dorothy watched them closely, sizing them up as parents of the missing girls. In her hand she held the photograph of Doreen Carlucci. She had seen plenty of cases in which parents had lost children due to negligence. The world was full of negligent parents, Dorothy knew; but such was not the case with Doreen's and Joanne's parents.

Francis Carlucci handed Dorothy some articles belonging to Doreen. Dorothy took a little gold bracelet in her hand, feeling it with her entire being. She felt sad as she held the precious possession and saw, without commenting to the families, the brutalized bodies of their little girls. She saw clearly that the girls were dead.

Tears began to form in her eyes as Dorothy heard from Francis that the bracelet had been a confirmation gift from Doreen's grandmother, whom she called Nanny. Dorothy thought of her own grandchildren, Sam's children, and how she loved to give them presents. A single clover leaf gleamed from the chain-link bracelet, "Love, Poppy and Nanny" inscribed on the back.

Dorothy knew she had to divert the parents' attention from too morbid thoughts. She swallowed, suppressing the tears.

Can't let them get depressed, she thought to herself. She remembered how her mother had taken traumatic situations into hand with a sudden change in mood, steering people away from their tragedies. Dorothy knew she had to reach for something to destroy the prevailing mood.

Dorothy looked at Vicaro. "Hey, Vic, who was that I saw you with the other night?" Dorothy suddenly called across the room.

Vic blushed. "Where're you talking about?" he asked.

"You can't hide from me, I know I saw you with someone the other night," Dorothy joked.

His face reddened; he knew there was no escaping Dorothy's vision. Everyone laughed as the suave cop realized the only person he had been with was his wife, Maryanne.

"I didn't say who I saw you with," Dorthy laughed. "I saw you with your wife, you guilty bastard."

Before they settled down to more direct questioning, Dorothy and the policeman told stories that had occurred over the years while they had worked together. As soon as Dorothy saw Francis and Jeannette relaxed and smiling, she knew it was time to get to work. She began to concentrate.

At first, in Dorothy's mind, the glow of silver metal seemed to radiate in the sun. She saw large metal boxes in a row. As she got closer, the boxes grew and she saw they were like vans. Five rows of metal vans stood next to what looked to be a wooded area.

As she described what she was seeing, Vicaro said, "Probably a trailer camp."

"That sounds right," Dorothy agreed. "I think it is a trailer camp."

"Is that where the girls are hidden?" Joe Carlucci asked.

"It's hard to tell," Dorothy said. "I don't get them in one of those trailers. They are nearby, somewhere, though."

Shoes. She saw shoes, both as a cartoon and as real shoes. Nurse's shoes. Soft white shoes and glistening stockings. She saw a woman, her face indistinguishable, in a nurse's uniform.

"These shoes bother me. So does the nurse," Dorothy said. "I can't figure them in this, but somewhere along the line they'll be involved. Maybe just in the area where you live."

After dinner Justine and Bob helped set out coffee and dessert for the families. Dorothy began to see things more clearly.

The trailer camp was in sharper focus, and she pinpointed one trailer with blue and silver coloring. But the words "silver" and "trailer" seemed significant in themselves. And the letters "m-e-a-d" appeared in conjunction with the camp.

"I don't know what it means, but I see the word 'silver' and the word 'mead,' like on a sign. Also the number 'nine' is important. Does any of this make any sense to you?" She looked at the parents, hoping for some indication of recognition. But none came.

"You're going to find the girls," she said slowly, in the manner of a pronouncement, "within the next three days. Probably tomorrow or the next day.

"I know it's rough, but let's work together in finding those two children." She sat between the two mothers, speaking forcefully, trying to support them in their grief.

After awhile Dorothy bounced up and looked at the clock. It was nearing midnight and she still wanted time alone to work on the girls' charts. She felt the presence of death inside her, and she knew from years of experience that she could not let it destroy her, as it nearly had with Michael Kurscics. She would not fall prey to the emotions being generated around her.

After talking with Vic, Dorothy suggested to the parents that they call the Woodbridge police with the clues Dorothy had given them.

"Maybe they can make heads or tails of it. They ought to, for all they haven't done yet," Dorothy suggested.

Francis Carlucci called the detective she had been dealing with and gave him the information about the trailer camp and the descriptions Dorothy gave of the area; Dorothy listened on another extension, finishing the conversation by mixing force with expletives. She feared the police would do nothing with the clues Francis Carlucci had asked them to pursue.

It would take twenty minutes for one of those cops to locate that trailer park, if they wanted to, she thought to herself. I'm going to have to find another way of locating that place.

That night Dorothy slept fitfully.
Once again she "spirited" in search of the resolution,

hunting for facts not yet disclosed, for landmarks that would help locate the two slain bodies she saw in the underbrush.

This time, in contrast to her experience with the Michael Kurscics case, Dorothy was in command. She saw the faces of the girls, wracked with the agony of final fear. Though saddened by the sight, the psychic was not as vulnerable as she once had been; now she moved upward, like a spiraling hawk cutting the chilly night with determination in its helix path. Around and around the landscape seemed to turn, as her eye searched for landmarks on which to prey.

The unfamiliar land seemed covered by spongelike darkness. Trees blanketed the ground. Light gently shimmered over a large area. As she aimed for the light, the area began to take a more definite shape. She saw a metallic glow, not shiny like glass, but softer, like a brushed metal reflecting the moon's glow. Lines took the form of square shapes. Row after row of metal rectangles. Dorothy knew she had found the trailer park.

She focused closer in search of landmarks. Now she could see the long low sign made of cinder blocks, with the word "silvermead" on it.

Down through a dark vein running through the woods she moved, undaunted by the darkness that harbored the bodies of the two victims no one else could see. Past where the girls lay, on and on through the serpentine artery, she silently glided until she reached a crossing of channels and a building. It was a small office structure. The mind's periscoping eye saw "Goldstein lawyer." Dorothy fell into a deep slumber.

The next morning Dorothy called the Carluccis. While she had prepared breakfast, the word "silvermead" continued to come to her, as did the vision of the trailers. Now, however, she felt that the "Goldstein" of her dream was also connected with the trailer camp.

"Goldstein? Who is he? Where is he?" Francis asked Dorothy.

"You know I can't tell directions very well, but I see him out at a crossroad somewhere about a mile or so from these trailers. Maybe a couple of towns below you, heading for Florida," Dorothy conjectured.

With the description and direction given by Dorothy, Joe Carlucci acted decisively. He phoned his brother-in-law, Tom Barbuda, in Freehold, which was in the direction indicated by Dorothy, and asked him to drive with him.

The two men spent hours driving around. Finally, after questioning people along the way, a lawyer's office was found that fit Dorothy's description.

Joe Carlucci entered the small, single-level office building and asked the receptionist if he might have a word with a lawyer named Goldstein.

"Do you have an appointment with Mr. Goldstein?" the young girl inquired.

"No, this is not really a business matter. I was sent here by a psychic and I need to see if Mr. Goldstein can help me with some information."

Confused, the secretary went into the office and came out with a short, middle-aged man who introduced himself to Joe Carlucci as Goldstein. The two men went into the lawyer's office where Joe sat down and eyed the small, prefabricated office.

The desperate father briefly explained what had brought him to the lawyer's office. As soon as Joe mentioned that a psychic had sent him, the balding lawyer indicated that his time was valuable and that he didn't believe in psychics. Not until Joe told him the psychic had pinpointed him and said that he might be able to decipher the words "silver" and "mead" and some connection to trailers, did Goldstein remove his wire-rim glasses and focus on the man sitting before him.

"Silvermead?" the incredulous lawyer stammered. "Are you saying 'Silvermead' as one word?"

"Any way you want it, I'll take it," Joe said.

"How does this psychic know me?" the lawyer asked.

"She doesn't. She doesn't even know where you are," Joe told him, confusing the lawyer even more.

The lawyer swiveled in his desk chair and looked at the three diplomas on the wall. "I know where she's talking about. I own a trailer there," he said as if talking to himself. "But not many people know I have it, since my name's not on it and I don't live there."

"Listen, Mr. Goldstein, I don't care what you do in your trailer, or why you have it. That you have a trailer is what I'm glad to hear. Just tell me where this camp is. My daughter is supposed to be near there."

Goldstein walked Joe outside and pointed to the right, down a road leading into a wooded area. "The camp is called Silvermead Trailer Park and you'll run into it about a mile and a half down the road."

Joe was heartened by the finding of Goldstein, although he didn't know what connections to make between his daughter and the lawyer. All he could do was follow his instincts with the details Dorothy had given the day before. She had mentioned a trailer that was blue and silver, so the two men headed down Route 9 for the Silvermead Trailer Camp in hopes of a resolution.

The trailer-camp entrance was a dirt road off to the left of a heavily wooded area. The mobile homes lined up in five rows formed an odd community, situated in an isolated area. The two men parked the car at the entrance and walked around the ground, looking for anything that might trigger a response or connection to Dorothy's clues. Each person they met was questioned and shown the photographs of the two adolescents.

After they had walked through the area and felt nothing more could be done, they drove around to diners and supermarkets to show people the photographs of the girls. The hours slipped away until the sun began to set and Joe Carlucci sighed with sadness and disappointment.

He believed in Dorothy, and he was frustrated that the police had evidently refused to consider her clues as a possibility.

As they drove north on Pergolaville Road toward Tom Barbuda's house, a screaming ambulance flared past them, going in the opposite direction. Joe was frightened that the sirens might be heading for his daughter. After leaving his brother-in-law at his home, Joe drove north quietly and slowly, sad at the thought of facing his hopeful wife.

Thirty minutes after Tom Barbuda had finished telling his wife of their afternoon encounters with Goldstein and the Silvermead Trailer Park, the phone rang. It was the Manalapan Police Department. The bodies of two girls had been found in the underbrush alongside Pergolaville Road by a bicyclist at around 4:00 P.M. No positive identification of the girls had been made. Could he pick up Joe Carlucci and bring him to Monmouth Medical Center for possible identification?

"Be prepared for an unpleasant sight," the lieutenant warned Tom. "These girls are in bad shape."

The eighteen-year-old bicyclist had spotted one of the girls lying faceup about ten feet off the road. When the police arrived, the second girl was found some ten feet away. One girl was wearing only work shoes, while the other had on a sweater and shoes.

The two men were led into the basement morgue of the hospital, where the air was chilly and the click of their heels resonated. The bodies lay rigid on steel tables covered by white starched fabric. Frightened by the sight of death and the moment of possible resolution, the two men moved with trepidation toward the tables where a hospital attendant stood waiting to show them the corpses.

Tom Barbudo held onto his brother-in-law while the sheet was removed, revealing Joe's daughter, Doreen. Brutality and death had worked an ugly alchemy on the girl; her flesh showed bruises that spread over much of her body.

"Yes," the weakened man moaned. "This is my daughter."

The other body was quickly identified as Joanne Delardo, and the two men left the room to breathe and regain their strength.

Medical Examiner Dr. Edwin Albano and a police detective sat with the saddened father. The examiner said that the bodies were "very cold" and had probably been "outside for some time." Curiously the area in which the girls were found had been searched earlier that week and no bodies had been discovered then. The Manalapan policeman said "they had to have been dumped there sometime yesterday afternoon."

"I don't know if you noticed the marks on your daughter's neck," the examiner continued, "but they are strangulation marks. A rubber-coated electrical cord was used to strangle the two girls. The cord was found around Joanne's neck."

The time of death was estimated to be at least ten days before but the doctor said "they could have been killed shortly after they disappeared sixteen days ago." A vaginal-semen test had been run and had proven negative: neither girl had been sexually molested.

Finally Joe asked exactly where the girls had been found. The policeman took out a map and showed him the spot indicated by a circle on the map.

"Is that anywhere near the Silvermead Trailer Camp?" the father inquired.

The policeman pointed to an area directly behind the circle. "Not more than a half a mile away, I'd say," the policeman estimated.

Joe looked at his brother-in-law in amazement.

"Did you have an ambulance with sirens going to pick up the girls, around four-thirty this afternoon?" Tom Barbuda asked.

The policeman thought for a moment. "That's about right. And yes, the dude had his sirens going."

Arrangements were made to have the bodies moved north to Colonia for burial preparations, and Joe and Tom left, both feeling numb from the experience.

While the police departments of Woodbridge and Manalapan met to exchange facts and organize material, the area in which the girls were found was combed thoroughly by police and hounds. Woodbridge Police Chief Anthony O'Brien said the officials had no leads or suspects in the case.

Francis Carlucci called Dorothy and told her that the girls had been identified in Manalapan Township, in an area very much like the one described in her vision.

"I would like to come down for the mass," Dorothy said. "I would also like to see where the girls were found."

While the girls' bruised bodies were prepared for the funeral, friends and relatives gathered together in the Carlucci living room. Dorothy sat with the family, helping them cope with the tragedy. While she sat talking with people, she again saw in her mind the uniform of a nurse.

Then she saw two men, one very tall, one of medium height. The taller man seemed considerably younger than the other man. Dorothy spoke with Francis in private.

"Maybe you're seeing me," Francis said. "I'm a nurse, and you said Thursday that you saw a nurse. I figured it was me."

"No," Dorothy insisted. "The nurse still bothers me. So do the shoes I keep seeing. There's something odd about those shoes."

Francis jumped up and went to a drawer in the china closet, pulling out several sheets of paper. Out of the pile she handed Dorothy a single piece of paper on which a cartoon of three pairs of feet and shoes were drawn.

"Are these the shoes?" Francis asked.

Dorothy smiled. "These are the shoes I saw before when you came to my house. Now I see different shoes. Who made this?"

"Doreen. The night she was killed. This was on the kitchen counter when the girls left for the Delardos."

"I think I see the men who killed your daughter," Dorothy said to Francis. "I keep seeing two men. The shorter one is middle-aged, heavyset, with a face that could kill. The taller one is younger, wears glasses, has a buck-tooth smile like a beaver. Does that sound familiar?"

No one recognized the men Dorothy saw. As they rode to Manalapan and the wooded area where the bodies had been found, Joe Carlucci pointed out Goldstein's office. Dorothy smiled, thinking how she must have unsettled the unsuspecting lawyer.

"He probably thinks that I know what he does in that trailer of his," Dorothy laughed. "You should have told him I was a friend of his wife. That would have made him think for awhile."

Dorothy got very strong feelings again about the nurse and the shoes.

"I know I see that nurse and those shoes. There's something going on around here that involves a nurse. You'll see."

As no one, including the police, could make sense of her descriptions, the matter was dropped. Dropped by everyone but Dorothy.

The next day, on her birthday, Dorothy received a phone call from Elaine DeMars. The woman had read about Dorothy in the papers, and about her involvement with finding the body of murdered schoolteacher Phyllis Thompson the previous year. Dorothy had not read about John DeMars's disappearance in the *Nutley Sun*. Elaine DeMars wanted to pay a visit to Dorothy—that day, if possible.

The desperate wife also told Deputy Chief Dimichino that she wanted Dorothy Allison brought in on the case. Dimichino was frustrated. A cop for twenty-nine years, he felt obsessed by the case, which after two weeks ranked as one of the most intensive searches in the history of the middle-class community of thirty-two thousand people.

Dimichino had heard of the Nutley psychic, and knew of Vicaro's involvements with her over the years. He wasn't a believer, but as nothing else had proven fruitful, he would send a detective to the Allisons' on Monday to talk with the woman.

Elaine DeMars and her mother-in-law went to Dorothy's on Sunday morning, ringing her doorbell at 8:00 A.M. The women were alarmed by the frightening reception they received from Jason, Dorothy's black German shepherd. Unsettled by the mastiff's greeting, they then found themselves at the mercy of a fast-moving psychic.

Dorothy set out coffee cups and plates for pastries, while the two well-dressed women nervously looked around at the Formica kitchen. Dorothy showed them her Capricorn stockings commemorating the day, her birthday.

"Don't tell me a thing about your husband or anything about what the police have done. Let me ask you questions first," Dorothy instructed them.

Again Dorothy saw the same two men she had seen the previous day while at the Carlucci house.

"Who's this funny-looking tall man with the long face and thick glasses and buck teeth? Ugly man, with another fatter, older man. The other one reminds me of a priest. Maybe he was once a priest or something in the church."

Elaine DeMars began to cry. Her mother-in-law took

her hand and told her to compose herself. Then the older woman turned to Dorothy.

"Why are you describing these men?" she asked.

"I don't know. Somehow I think they are connected to this case," Dorothy explained.

"Well, your description sounds very like my missing son, John, and my son-in-law, Brian. He's a lay deacon for the diocese in Paterson, so maybe that's why you saw the priest's robes."

Dorothy began to laugh. "Believe it or not," she said, "I described your son to the Woodbridge police yesterday as the murderers of Doreen Carlucci. Isn't that funny?"

Only Dorothy laughed at the fact that she had not only seen John DeMars and his brother-in-law prior to meeting the two women, but that she had misinterpreted them as murderers.

Dorothy was able to change the subject quickly. She saw how unhappy John DeMars's mother was with what she had said.

"Have faith," Dorothy told the woman. "I've been looking for people for eight years now, and I've been very successful. I know I get my cases confused a lot of the time. I can't even read a map. It just happens that I pick up things that may have something to do with a case I'm working on elsewhere, or in the future. Imagine how confusing it is for me.

"When I was out in Pennsylvania last summer," the psychic continued, "I told the police to watch for an airplane that was yellow and silver and had something to do with Yankee Doodle Dandy. I said it was a small plane and that something was going to happen to it in the nearby area. I wasn't sure it had anything to do with the case I was working on, but I knew the plane was in trouble. The next day a plane crashed in the next town. It was July Fourth and the plane was the Yankee Tripper. Who knew?

"I see a woman with white hair," Dorothy said, getting down to business and focusing on John DeMars. "I think she's in an office. She would have had something to do with your husband, probably at the bank. Her name is Margaret."

101

Elaine DeMars said nothing, but she knew that the white-haired woman Dorothy described did work at the Chemical Bank and her name was Margaret. She listened closely to everything Dorothy said.

Dorothy poured coffee all around, giving orange juice to Paul and Justine, who sat listening to the fate of the Nutley man whose disappearance was also being discussed at school. The police, everyone knew, had come up with very little.

While her children talked with the two women, Dorothy saw an arrow flying across the sky, zooming against a sky-blue backdrop. As if propelled of its own accord, the arrow glided and began to descend. Water. Dorothy saw water and she knew that John DeMars had drowned.

She looked at the two women. The young wife was anxiously listening to her every word, watching her closely as if scrutinizing her facial movements for possible clues as to what was going on inside the psychic's head.

"Mrs. DeMars, did your husband ever suffer from amnesia?" Dorothy asked.

"No, not that I know of," she replied, and her mother-in-law nodded her head in agreement.

"I do see your husband, I can't say where or when right now, but I do see him. I think he had something like amnesia. I really can't tell. He's moving, and yet he's not. I see him sleeping or unconscious, but still in a suit and still alive. Your husband wore a suit to work everyday, didn't he?"

"Yes," the woman said.

"I'm getting a glimpse of him *before* he ran into trouble. Why don't you give me today to think and tomorrow we'll talk about it. Today is a national holiday in this house, so I'm gonna unplug this thing," she said, pointing to her head, "and be with my family."

"I appreciate your helping," Elaine DeMars extended her hand. "I have asked the police to involve you in the investigation. Please work with them. I just know you can find my husband."

Dorothy gave the woman a warm hug and told her to rest, that her husband would be found. She didn't say, however, whether he would be dead or alive.

As the two women walked out the door, Dorothy stopped them. "Does your husband take the same train home everyday? I mean, he's usually regular, right?"

"Clockwork. His life is like clockwork," Elaine DeMars replied. "Everyday he rides the same train from Hoboken. Almost without fail, unless the trains are broken down, or there's something on the line."

"On the line," Dorothy repeated. "I've got a feeling there is something on the line. Have the police investigated the train?"

The anxious young wife assured Dorothy that the police had interviewed hundreds of people, including commuters and all the train personnel. Mrs. DeMars told her nothing had come of the investigations. People had recognized her husband, but no one could swear he had gotten on the train that night.

"Someone is swearing wrong, I think. I'll talk to the police. Good-bye," and Dorothy closed the door.

On Monday morning Deputy Chief Dimichino called Detective Lubertazzi into his office.

"You've got an appointment this morning," Dimichino told Lupo. "Call this lady and tell her what time you're going over to talk with her."

Lupo took the paper and read the name "Allison" and a phone number. "What's this about?" Lupo asked.

"The DeMars case. This woman says she sees him," Dimichino said, trying not to give away too much.

"Sees or saw?" Lupo asked again.

"Sees." The deputy chief smiled behind his cigarette.

"You're not serious about this, are you? I'm not going to work with some nut who says she sees John DeMars. Why not get one of the religious nuts to meet her? This is a joke, right?"

"This is no joke, and you're going to talk to her this morning whether or not you like it. Elaine DeMars was at her house yesterday and she called me at home to say that this Allison woman sees her husband. So what am I supposed to say?" Dimichino paused. "This is the woman Vicaro worked with on the Kurscics case. We've got nothing more to lose than an hour of your goddamn time, right?"

Dimichino demanded, standing before the quiet cop and staring him down. "I suggest you move your ass and call her before Mrs. DeMars and her Knight of Columbus brother-in-law come down here and knock it out of you."

Lupo shrugged his shoulders and turned away, muttering to himself in Italian.

Lupo had never met a psychic. He had heard about the Nutley woman from the other cops, but Vicaro, having been the focus of some derision, kept his dealings with Dorothy fairly quiet. Lupo was nervous. He even felt nauseated as he phoned the woman and told her he would be at her house in forty-five minutes.

"Come right in if I don't get to the door. I may have my hands in dough, so answering the door may be hard," Dorothy cheerfully told the cop.

Lupo first tried to find Vicaro, but the other policeman was in Newark transporting a criminal. Lupo thought of what he knew about psychics. Pictures of turbaned swamis in white robes made him even more nervous. He decided, while he drove to Dorothy's, that if she wore huge black earrings and played organ music, he would leave and lie to Dimichino. Lupo felt like a child going into a haunted house for the first time.

He parked the squad car on the steep incline in front of Dorothy's house and looked at the two-story white and brown house ensconced in bushes and trees. He took in a deep breath and walked up the steps to the front door. A large black dog barked angrily in the window to the right of the door, giving Lupo a stare that made him want to turn around. A second later an attractive woman in black slacks and a white silk blouse with sleeves rolled up to the elbow answered the door.

She looked at the shy green eyes and brush moustache of the detective in his tan suit.

"What's the matter? You cops afraid of a sweet dog? I thought you guys could handle them." Dorothy led Lupo into the den, tossing his overcoat on the sofa. "Come into the kitchen while I finish this bread. Then we can have some for lunch."

Lupo sat down at the Formica table and looked in wonder at the woman claiming to see John DeMars. His eye

104

wandered over the stacks of newspapers and police data in the dining room.

"Looks like headquarters. How come you've got so much police stuff around? You in business?" Lupo asked.

"Business? Are you kidding? That's what my husband wants to know. Am I in business. I'm not like all those other money-hungry psychics. I got something most people don't have, and I don't think it's right to charge. Saint Anthony doesn't charge for finding kids," Dorothy said.

"Listen, Mrs. Allison," Lupo tried to get her attention, "I can't stay all day. I've got other people to talk to this afternoon."

"No one is going to tell you where the body is, but me," Dorothy challenged him. "No one you're going to talk to this afternoon will be able to help. So sit there and be quiet for a minute, or I'll stuff you," and she laughed.

Lupo had never met anyone like Dorothy. He was intimidated, at the mercy of this unusual woman.

While Dorothy cleaned and rinsed dishes that were scattered around her kitchen, images began to appear in her mind. An arrow soared across the sky, slowly descending to earth. The arrow landed in underbrush, which seemed to be along the shore of a river. Dorothy sensed water all around.

"I'm gonna tell you from the start," Dorothy said to the cop, "your man is dead. That banker was great with loans and money, but he wasn't so careful with himself. He's dead, and you're going to find him in water."

Lupo sipped steaming hot coffee and jotted notes as Dorothy spoke. He wasn't sure what he could ask her, or what he could expect from her. Dorothy, growing more accustomed to police work and jargon, knew how to be direct with investigators. Lupo merely took down what she said.

"The most important thing right now is that someone you've already interrogated hasn't told you the full story. When you find out the rest, it will change the whole case for you. You'll probably find out about it today or tomorrow."

"Who was this person?" Lupo asked.

"I'm not sure. It's not anyone in the family. I see some-

105

one in a uniform, like yours. But he's not a cop. He's some other type of official. Go down your list of people you've talked to and see who wears that kind of uniform. It might be a train conductor," Dorothy concluded.

The arrow, as Dorothy could see it from above, was not far from a row of old tires, scattered in a line on the ground. She could make out the numbers "166" in the far distance, and then, in a different way, the numbers "222" appeared.

"Look for the numbers 'one, six, six' and 'two, two, two' around the body. They don't have anything to do with each other, and they might not be places," she warned him, and then added, "I see a playground, too."

Dorothy made him a turkey and ham sandwich and stayed with her psychic periscoping at the same time.

"I see that arrow and archer again," she said.

"What do you suppose archery has to do with John De-Mars?" Lupo asked.

"I can't tell. There might be an archery range nearby, or maybe he was killed accidentally by a flying Indian with a bow and arrow." Dorothy looked over at the cop to see if he had taken down her little joke. He was looking at her, wondering what she meant by a "flying Indian."

"You'd be a horse's ass if you'd taken that down," Dorothy laughed. "Relax, I'm not going to fly across the room."

Dorothy began to catalog her details. "I see the playground, tires, two guys, and a place that looks like a plant or factory that has burned down. You know, like charred slabs of concrete. Does any of that mean anything to you?"

"What the hell are two guys in a playground supposed to tell me?" the cop demanded.

"I didn't say there were two guys in a playground. I don't know what it means, either. It might not be two people," Dorothy explained. "I don't always know what I'm seeing. I never know where I am or in what direction I'm going. You've got to know that. I may say head for Mexico meaning walk thirty yards in that direction. When you find DeMars's body, you'll see that all these things are around him."

Lupo's green eyes bulged like an inquisitive mantis's. He didn't know what to think of the list before him. He knew he wasn't going to show it to anyone at the police station, nor would he consider discussing it with anyone. The skeptic in him stood his ground.

"This last weekend I looked for two kids down below Colonia," Dorothy told him. "Two little murdered teenagers. How I hate those murderers." Tears came to her eyes, and her voice got louder. "If I could get my hands on these bastards who did it, I'd strangle them and call it self-defense. As long as I'm alive, I'll try to get a picture of the bastard that murdered those girls."

Lupo was moved by the feelings Dorothy exhibited. The thought of the short woman attacking thugs and getting away with it amused him, however. He felt certain she could do it.

"I'll bet you could get them, too," Lupo said.

"Damn right I would. One of these days I have a feeling you and I are going to have just that opportunity. I have a feeling you and I are going to work together on another case, more important than this one."

Lupo wasn't sure whether he was pleased or nervous about Dorothy's prediction. For the time being he wanted to get out of her house and be alone. He thanked Dorothy for her help and sandwiches and told her that if anything came of the clues, he would let her know.

"Listen, *paesan*. Between us, I don't think you believe a word I'm saying." Her large brown eyes challenged him. "That's fine with me. Just don't waste my time coming back if you're not going to check into those clues. You tell Mrs. DeMars to leave me alone if you're not going to take me seriously. Okay?" Dorothy challenged him.

Lupo blushed. He managed to stammer a farewell and a promise to be in touch. With that, he was out the door and hurrying to his car.

Back at his desk Lupo quietly went over the clues given to him by the psychic. A row of tires. That could be any dumping ground. What two guys and what park?

Maybe the two guys are archers. Or underwater divers with spears. Lupo's mind reeled with possibilities.

In the meantime dozens of calls and reports from around the metropolitan New York area came in from people claiming to have seen DeMars. Cabdrivers, postal workers, commuters, convenience store managers called in reporting that someone looking exactly like DeMars had just been seen.

The most important call of the day came from a Lyndhurst resident. The caller, who wouldn't give his name, was a bond broker in Manhattan. He reported that he was a regular commuter on the Erie Lackawanna, and that he got off each evening in Lyndhurst, the stop just before Nutley. He had seen the articles in the papers about the Chemical Bank officer and recognized him as one of the nightly commuters.

On the night in question the anonymous broker reported that he had absentmindedly missed his own stop in Lyndhurst. He said that he had asked the conductor to stop the train because he had missed his stop. The train had only moved forward a hundred feet or less and was brought to a quick stop.

"It was very dark outside," the man told Lupo, "and there was no light when I looked out the doors when the train stopped again. We were probably a hundred feet away from the Lyndhurst station, on the train bridge over the Passaic," the broker reported. "I decided it was too dark and too far to walk back to the station, so I went back to my seat and waited for Nutley." When he got back to his seat, the man next to him offered to drive him to Lyndhurst.

"In any case, anyone could have gotten off that train mistakenly," the voice conjectured. "You ought to check with the train officials," he suggested and then hung up.

Lupo could not evade the fact that Dorothy's words of the morning might have come true. If the man's call was legitimate, then someone on that train was not telling the truth, because someone had to have stopped it.

At the railway office Lupo tracked down the conductor and one of the engineers from the train DeMars had usually taken out of Hoboken. This time, with the bond broker's report in hand, plus Dorothy's warnings in the back of his mind, he interrogated the two men for the third time in three weeks.

As the engineer recaptured the scene, he recalled that a businessman in the third car had run to him just after they left the Lyndhurst station and asked him to stop the train. The commuter had missed his stop.

"Isn't that unusual, to make an extra stop?" Lupo asked.

The engineer, a man in his thirties, nodded in agreement.

"Why didn't you tell me about this man before?" Lupo asked.

"Your picture of DeMars and the man who asked me to stop the train aren't the same person," the engineer defended himself. "I never saw DeMars that night."

"That's the problem," Lupo said. "No one can place him on the train that night. At least, not yet. I can see we'll have to jar a few more memories." Lupo gave each man a final stare and left.

Lupo called Dorothy and told her that he had found the missing part of the story.

"The train made an extra stop over the Passaic," he told her. "What do you think?"

"I think you should pick me up tomorrow and we should start looking for his body along the river," she suggested. "If that's okay with you, I'll cancel my hair appointment."

"I'll pick you up around ten o'clock," Lupo said.

"What's the matter, you busy at nine?" Dorothy asked.

"No, I just thought . . . ," Lupo stammered.

"Pick me up at nine. The earlier the better. See you tomorrow," and she disconnected.

Based on the suspicion that DeMars was on the train, although that fact had not been proved, and on the fact that the train had made an extra stop on the bridge, Lupo suggested to Dimichino that the Passaic be thoroughly checked.

"It's mighty cold out there." Dimichino rolled his eyes. "I'll tell the chief and he can call the Essex County divers for help. I'll tell him you're going too, floating on your psychic," Dimichino laughed and walked away.

Lupo was not willing to believe so readily in Dorothy's powers. That the men "in uniforms" had been found might have been coincidence. He was going to check out everything that came over the transom, hoping to counter her predictions.

For three days, eight hours a day, Lupo joined the Essex County divers under the train trestle in the cold Passaic. Dorothy walked along the swampy, rubbish-ridden banks, trying to ascertain which way DeMars's body had gone. She was certain that he had been on the train and had suffered some sort of amnesia which caused him to leap unwittingly to his death.

Through mud and sludge, along the banks of the Passaic, Dorothy trampled in knee-high boots and a pink ski parka with a fluffy white hood. Their hope was to catch the body before it traveled to Newark Bay. The pair ceaselessly worked together tracking down clues and interpreting Dorothy's feelings. Three days of diving and swimming in the river proved fruitless, but left Lupo with a case of influenza.

Four days later, after Lupo regained his strength, he and another cop chased down reports that DeMars had been jogging in Newark. It took two days to track down the jogger, who resembled the missing man only from the rear. Another report came from a taxi driver who swore he had picked up DeMars at the Lyndhurst station on the day in question and left him at Newark Airport. Two days of questioning dozens of people at Newark Airport proved fruitless.

Lupo was still unwilling to believe totally in Dorothy. He chased a caller's clues from Long Branch, New Jersey, a city forty miles south of Nutley on the Jersey shore, with dogged tenacity. So positive was he that DeMars would be found in Long Branch that he dragged Dorothy down to the Seven Eleven store where the pair stood for two days talking to customers and passing out pictures of DeMars. The caller insisted that he had seen him; none of the convenience store shoppers recognized the six-foot-three man with wire-rim glasses. So far Dorothy had been more right than wrong.

Everyday Lupo stopped at the DeMars home and reported the findings of the detectives working on the case. Dimichino was frustrated, the chief was angry, and the detectives felt their angst. From day one, DeMars's deacon brother-in-law had called out the Knights of Columbus to assist in the investigation. More and more they got on the police department's nerves, raveling and unraveling details that had been gone over time and again.

To add to Dimichino's frustration, the New York *Daily News* ran an article on January 13 entitled, "Nutley Cops Draw a Blank on Missing Banker." Chief Buel was angered and embarrassed by the article, and he let his men know his feelings.

By late January, Lupo and Dorothy had traveled back and forth along the riverbanks in the vicinity of the Lyndhurst stop dozens of times. Dorothy began to feel that searching any more was futile. Then the numbers "222" came to her again and she told Lupo that he should hold onto those numbers. They would be important.

That night Dorothy called Lupo at home and told him that DeMars would not be found until February 22. She had decided that was the meaning of the numbers.

"I don't think we should search anymore. Don't be like that crazy Vicaro who wouldn't believe me when I gave him a date and he told me I should keep searching anyway," Dorothy warned. "I've got other cases I'm working on, too, so I better give them a little more attention. They're kids, and I think they need my help more than this banker."

"You mean we just sit around till the twenty-second? What am I going to tell the DeMars family?" Lupo wondered.

"Tell them you're following leads and trailing down clues like always. You police know how to lie better than anyone. You won't have any problems," Dorothy laughed. "The only thing that will bring him up sooner than that date will be those Knights of Columbus. Maybe they'll bless him so much the river will choke and spit him up."

Lupo was surprised at Dorothy's humor, but before he could respond, she had disconnected.

Two days later Dorothy received a call from the Woodbridge police. They wanted to visit her for a little while that afternoon. Dorothy made herself available to them.

Two police detectives arrived around 3:00 P.M. They reported to Dorothy that they still had no leads in the Carlucci-Delardo murders. The only suspect was in jail for

111

the murder of a teen-ager in a community not far from Colonia. Nothing, however, would link him to the two girls.

Dorothy asked the two men if they had any suspects who had anything to do with shoes or shoemaking, who might have raped or murdered a woman. Probably a nurse.

The older man asked Dorothy if she had read any of the recent reports about Joseph Kallanger. Dorothy seldom read the newspapers or listened to television. She relied on her family to point her toward pertinent news. Dorothy had not heard of Kallanger.

A shoemaker from Philadelphia, Joseph Kallanger, with the aid of his teen-age son, had raped and brutally murdered a nurse in Leonia, New Jersey, on January 8. In a case that would stun and frighten people everywhere, the story of Joseph Kallanger took months to unravel, while a growing number of female victims in Pennsylvania, Delaware, and New Jersey were attributed to him, many only on speculation.

Dorothy was sickened to discover the source of the shoes and the nurse that had haunted her. She felt, however, that the man the detective spoke of had nothing to do with the murdered girls.

Dorothy sensed an unfriendly air about the two cops. It took her only a moment to realize what they had on their mind.

"Mrs. Allison, would you answer a few questions for us? You seem to know an awful lot about this case and we thought you might be able to help," the stern-looking detective said.

Dorothy asked if the Carluccis knew they were questioning her. The blond-haired, younger man said they had not been notified of the visit. That confirmed Dorothy's suspicions.

"Mrs. Allison, where were you the night of December thirteenth?"

"Listen, you guys, you can ask all the questions you want. I just want you to know that I think you're cheap, half-baked cops, and your handling of this entire investigation has been rotten." Her eyes glared with anger. "Now you're questioning someone who had never seen these peo-

112

ple till the day after Christmas, two weeks after the disappearance."

She stopped short for a moment and looked at the older man. "I can't tell you why I know you have a mentally retarded daughter," Dorothy said to him. "I just see it. Have you ever met me before?" she challenged him.

The man looked at his partner and told Dorothy he was amazed that she knew his daughter was retarded.

"Well, be amazed that I knew those two poor girls were murdered and would be found quickly, while you men insisted they'd run away. You cops certainly did nothing to make life easier for those two suffering families." Dorothy stood tall as she confronted the two men.

After fifteen minutes the two men left like puppies leaving an obedience school. Dorothy was angered at their reasoning, suspecting her of having any connection to the murder of two beautiful children. The saddest fact would be that the murderer of Doreen and Joanne was never to be found.

It was on February 22 that the Kearny Police Department phoned Lubertazzi in Nutley. The Kearny assistant detective reported that a body had been found in the Passaic River. A wallet had been found on the body, with Nutley identification inside.

"What's the name in the wallet?" Lupo asked.

"DeMars. I think we've found your man," the detective said in a congratulatory tone.

Lupo hopped into his car and drove the several miles to the site of the body as described by the Kearny cop.

Lupo parked his car in the dirt near the muddy shoreline of the Passaic River, five miles downstream from Nutley. He walked alongside the park and discovered that the body had been found some fifty feet behind a Two Guys department store. As he walked and mentally cross-checked the scene with Dorothy's vision, he was amazed by her accuracy. Here was the Two Guys department store, there the playground, and as he stood on the chalk-lined grave, he saw the charred ruins of what had been a paint factory across the river.

It was not until a few days later, when the railway

bridge next to the Lyndhurst station was investigated, that he saw the number "166" emblazoned on a tugboat that was permanently stationed under the bridge.

Lupo could see the tracks made by the coroner and all the policemen in the mud. He followed the tracks through to the park where a teen-aged boy watched him approach.

"Did they find anything else with the body?" the sixteen-year-old inquired.

Lupo explained that he was not part of the Kearny investigation, that he had only come down to see the place.

"Do you know how they found the guy?" Lupo inquired.

The boy's face lit up.

"Yeah, me and my Dad found him," he said proudly. "We were shooting arrows at a target, and one got away. I ran to chase it way down by the river's edge, and I saw that man's leg in the mud and plants. I ran back and my dad went over to Two Guys and called the police."

Lupo was stunned at the sight of the archer. "You've done terrific, kid. Keep it up."

Lupo walked to his car and drove to Dorothy's to share the news with her.

Chapter 5

December 3, 1976
Dear Detective Lubertazzi,

I read in the *Enquirer* about Mrs. Allison helping you with a case in 1975 in helping you to find two children.

I was wondering could you please help me get in touch with her to help me find my daughter. She has been gone since July 22, 1976. Our Police and State Police can't find a thing. It will soon be five months and I and my whole family are nearly out of our minds. Her name is: Debbie Kline, she was 19 November 28. She disappeared coming home from work. We found her new 76 Vega parked in the mud and thick bushes. Her pocket book and all her I. D. cards was in her billfold along with her money $30.00. *Please* help me if you can. I don't know what else we can do. *Please* call me at this no. collect anytime.

Please do not think this a prank or anything like that.

Please please help me. I have no place else to turn and it is terrible when you try everything and found nothing.

Please call as soon as possible.
Thank you very much
Mrs. Richard A. Kline, Sr.
Waynesboro, Pennsylvania

Waynesboro is a small, conservative, and Fundamentalist community forty miles southwest of the state capital, Harrisburg, and on the western perimeter of the Quaker Dutch country. Surrounded by green orchards and rolling farmlands, Waynesboro has one main street, one high school, and one hospital. The people of the town are television watchers and churchgoers: if churches were as easy to install as televisions, there might be many more houses of worship.

Waynesboro, and its close neighbor to the north, Chambersburg, exist in a pocket-size world all their own. It is said that during the Depression, people in the two communities hardly knew what all the fuss was about. Even tourists seldom find the bucolic area; Gettysburg and the Amish areas draw most of the traffic east of the towns.

Violent crimes seldom seem to occur in the two communities; most "crimes" there are deviations from accepted religious doctrine. Religious and community leaders work together to keep the towns on an event keel. Disturbing ideas and modern changes were kept at bay as much as possible by the strong Evangelical leaders throughout the area. The local newspapers, which are published in Chambersburg, became sounding boards for public battles against invading ideas or factions not welcomed by the resident faiths.

The Richard Kline family fit into the fabric of the area. Dick and Jane Kline had known the mountains and hills around their small comfortable home all their lives. As local folks, they had quietly tended to their own business, been respectful of God and country, and mindful of the needs of their six children.

The tall, blond-haired father had worked for the Waynesboro golf club since the age of twelve, and after twenty-eight years, still worked as the superintendent of the course. An easygoing, affable man, he and his wife had raised a Protestant family by making family concerns their priority, rather than religion. Nevertheless Dick Kline gave his children full opportunity to grow up with the church as moral backdrop.

Jane, his short, stout, graying wife, moved in the world

at a rocking-chair gait, the pace sometimes broken by moments of nervousness and fear. Jane cared and tended for her family with an eye out for the unexpected, even though it seldom visited them.

Eighteen-year-old Debbie Kline, the third of the Kline children, graduated from Waynesboro High School in May of 1976. Debbie, an average student, had matured quietly; she was not one to exhibit sudden enthusiasms or emotional changes. She had her senior ring, which she treasured so much that it was safely sequestered in her jewelry box, and she had her diploma.

The reticent brown-haired beauty had had one boyfriend, with whom she had broken up just prior to graduation. Most of her free time was spent to her family, and her strongest attachment was with her mother. Debbie would spend hours sitting beside her mother, leafing through magazines, quietly passing time.

Debbie summed up her life in a letter to a close friend by saying that "things are really starting to shape up. I got a job which I start in the beginning of July . . . I got a beautiful burgundy Vega with only thirteen miles on it . . . things are really looking good for me and I am enjoying every bit of it. I'm so happy . . ."

On Thursday, July 22, Debbie and her mother spent the morning thumbing through the Montgomery Ward catalog, looking for clothes that Debbie might wear at her sister's wedding in October. Like a winsome kitten, she played that rainy, warm morning with her mother and her two-year-old niece, who romped around the house in Debbie's white work shoes.

Later Debbie went off to work at Waynesboro Hospital, only five minutes from her home. She called her mother around 4:30 P.M. to say that she had been paid and that she wanted to take her father out for pizza when she got home—a surprise she knew he would like.

It had rained most of that day. The sky remained overcast during the afternoon and early evening. The trees and ferns were a deep, glistening green, while the dirt road in front of the Kline's house was a muddy stream. Late in the day Dick labored on their well-manicured lawn, tending flower beds and snipping weeds.

Debbie usually got home around 6:30. When she hadn't arrived by that time, Jane stuck her head out the screen door and asked Dick if he'd seen or heard from her. He hadn't.

"You can set time by her," Dick said. "Debbie's never late. Maybe she's having trouble with that new car."

At 6:45, Dick and Jane got in their car and drove down the quiet rural road alongside the golf course. Then, forking to the right, they rode through a shady Revolutionary-period neighborhood to the hospital.

Debbie's new Vega was not in the parking lot. Jane looked at her husband. Neither said a word. They drove the route Debbie usually took home, Jane's eyes darting in all directions, but they found nothing. Jane suggested the gas station, but no burgundy Vega was visible.

Next, back through the small town and on to a girl friend's home, where Debbie sometimes stopped to visit. She had not been there that afternoon. Jane Kline was showing signs of fear.

The couple headed back to their home via the same route. They passed a vacant lot where ten days before a minister's home, in the last days of construction, had burned to the ground. It was at the bottom of the hill below the Kline house. Jane noticed a township police car parked alongside the road. A lot of policemen had been in and around the razed site, so the Klines didn't think their presence odd.

As they passed the site, however, Jane turned around to look into the lot through a break in the high hedge of bushes, and she glimpsed a burgundy car.

Dick backed up instantly and they discovered that the car behind the bushes was Debbie's. Jane, now panic-stricken, took hold of her husband's arm for support. The policeman had been running a license check on the car, they learned, but it had proved futile, since the car was too new for the registration to have been processed.

Nowhere could they see their daughter. Frantic, Jane and Dick began searching the area. The sun, still penetrat-

118

ing the cumulus cloud cover, allowed plenty of light for seeing into the bushes and trees. No trace of their daughter was found. They checked the two-story shaft of the still-standing fireplace and chimney, a last, lonely appendage of the destroyed house, but found nothing.

How could Debbie have disappeared in daylight at the side of an often traveled residential road? The policeman, in words that would be repeated by uniformed men for the next several days, suggested that their daughter might have run away. Her parents knew she had not run away. It wasn't even a possibility.

For several grueling weeks the Kline family hunted everywhere a possibility sprouted. The vaguest clue, like a hiker's report that he had smelled rotting flesh at a spot high in the mountains, was pursued by Dick Kline. State and local police gathered what little they had to go on and interviewed anyone who had seen or known Debbie Kline.

A special phone installed by the Klines for information regarding Debbie's whereabouts proved both aggravating and fruitless. There were several crank calls, and others giving information that led only to disappointments and more sadness. One call came through that Jane believed was truthful. The whispering caller said nothing more than, "Debbie's dead," and hung up.

Prayer sessions and public search parties were organized as the small town's own speculative fears were increased by circulating rumors. Headlines during the first period of the investigation reveal the agonizing pace the investigation took: "Bloodhound Search Futile"; "Third Search Launched for Missing Girl"; "Quarry Search Proves Fruitless"; "Search for Debbie Enters Sixth Week." State police, headed by Sergeant Hussack, had tried everything within possibility.

"I don't think Debbie is going to come home alive," the frenzied mother told Marie Lanser of the *Public Opinion*, one of the two local newspapers. "In my mind I want Debbie home. I've got to see her, you know how you've got to see someone. But in my heart I don't think I'm going to see her."

The distraught mother recalled her daughter's perilous entry into the world. Debbie had been born two months prematurely at 5:13 A.M. on Thanksgiving morning, after Jane had begun to hemorrhage internally. For two months the helpless infant had hung precariously between life and death. That battle she had won.

"I sit in this room with my hand on the Bible and I pray," Jane said, rocking back and forth in her chair, bringing her hand to her tearing eyes.

"It's like a nightmare," the saddened father said. "You want to wake up, but you can't wake up. You watch things like this on television, but it doesn't happen to you."

"The nighttime's the worst," Debbie's twenty-four-year-old sister said. "You don't sleep."

"It's a small world when you're trying to hide," Dick said. "But it's a big world when a person's lost."

As the leaves on the trees began to color, and cooler weather eased in after the heat of August, the torment and anguish of the Kline family began to take its toll. Jane Kline became a recluse and spoke only through tears. Their children talked little, one sister often closing her door and crying herself into oblivion.

For the Kline family holidays took on a different meaning, as would the notion of giving thanks. By late October Jane and Dick had decided that Thanksgiving would go unheeded.

"We've got nothing to be thankful for," Jane said.

It was the desperation that fermented over months of waiting that led the quiet, small-town family to examine the idea of using a source never before considered: a psychic. In November the Klines contacted several people claiming to have psychic powers. One psychic from Chicago mailed tham a price sheet, demanding money before arrival. All the psychics they approached had a price. The Klines were willing to pay for further investigation, but money was not easy for them to find.

Eldon Joiner, a close friend and golf pro, offered to help the family out. The son of a highly regarded Southern criminal lawyer, the white-haired, lively Georgian had moved to the quiet area around Waynesboro in 1945. He had been a successful lawyer, made some money, and after changing jobs a few times, finally opted for the gentlemanly profession of golf. Though a staunch disbeliever in psychics, the family friend was willing to help them try anything.

The same day Lubertazzi received the letter from Jane Kline, he received a similar letter from a desperate mother in Florida whose daughter was reported missing on July 22, the same day Debbie Kline had vanished. All Dorothy's mail went to the Nutley Police Department. This method was used for her protection. Finding dead bodies was not particularly unsafe, but hunting murderers and rapists could jeopardize her life and the safety of her family. Consequently Dorothy's address and phone number were given out to few people. Lupo and his wife, Phyllis, would present Dorothy with the cases and requests, and according to her own schedule and the feelings she might get when looking over a case, she would choose which cases to work on.

Dorothy immediately grabbed both the Kline case and the one in Florida, feeling that "doubles" would play an important role in them. She believed that information she might give to the Klines would be pertinent to the Florida case.

When Dorothy phoned Jane Kline, she told the desperate mother that she would not be able to get to Waynesboro until some time after the New Year. With occasional visits made in connection with a Staten Island case, plus two other cases with which she was occupied, and a promised flight to Flordia to search for the missing twelve-year-old, her time was seldom her own. Over the past two years Dorothy's time had been consumed more and more by her work, which had long since taken on the fervency of a life's mission. Instead of three or four cases, she was handling up to ten cases at a time, some within the region, other via phone communication. Her dining room was stacked high with newspaper clippings and police photographs and data. Her phones, sitting side by side on the bookcase, would ring at all hours of the day or night, with calls giving her last minute details on cases or feedback from clues she had gotten psychically sitting at home in her den.

In addition to her pressing schedule, with the holidays and her own birthday imminent, Dorothy felt she must focus on her family for the next several weeks, trying to keep travel at a minimum.

Jane Kline offered to fly the psychic to nearby Harrisburg, but Dorothy refused, saying she would drive and save them the expense.

"I feel something very important is going to happen around the thirteenth of January," Dorothy told Jane. "I'm not sure what it is, but in the end it will make sense. Do you know any Richards?" Dorothy inquired.

"My whole family is Richards," Jane said nervously.

"How about a Robert or a Ronald? I'm looking for a man whose middle name is either Lee or Leroy. There will be double letters in the last name of one of the men," Dorothy predicted.

"One of the men?" Jane Kline queried.

"Yes, there are two men involved. Your daughter was with two men," Dorothy told her.

Dorothy proceeded to describe a car in the scene and an area where a building had burned recently. A building which she felt had belonged to a priest. A building with an outdoor oven standing.

Yellow. Dorothy said she saw a great burst of yellow. Not flowers, but something that was expansive and brightly painted.

"We need to find that yellow. It's important to where Debbie is right now," Dorothy said. "Also, have the police locate double bridges," Dorothy instructed, "because that's the route they took.

"Mrs. Kline, I'm going to give you some dates," Dorothy told her. "Please write them down and see if they have any meaning to your family. This will help me know if I'm on the right track." Dorothy gave Jane four dates: October 2, October 11, December 3, and April 4.

Dorothy received a call the next day from a Chambersburg reporter saying that he and another reporter would be available to her when she arrived in the area. The two veteran reporters, Bob Cox and photographer Ken Peiffer, saw the beginning of an exciting newspaper story, which two years later they would also publish as a book.

It was not until January 22 that Dorothy traveled with Bob and their son Paul to Waynesboro. It was on a cold, bitter Saturday that the trio drove the five and a half hours across Pennsylvania. They went first to Chambersburg, where they were met by the two *Record Herald* reporters. They, in turn, drove the Allisons to the Kline house, where the entire family sat waiting in suspense.

Dorothy's phone conversation had floored the grieving parents as they had instantly recognized some of Dorothy's clues. The burned house had to be the remains of the Moser house, where Debbie's car had been found. Moser, the Klines knew, was a minister, hence Dorothy's "priest" was nearly correct.

The dates Dorothy had offered had surprised the family, as well. Three of the dates were family wedding days, one of which Debbie had been planning to attend in October. The fourth date was important only to Debbie: in her journal it was the day highlighted for her first date with her boy-friend.

Dorothy arrived with a composite she had worked on with a Clifton, New Jersey, police artist. She had tried to see through the victim's eyes at the time of her struggle, hoping to have a picture of at least one of the perpetrators of the crime she knew to have taken place. When she met Dick Kline, however, she was startled. The composite she held in her hand looked like him.

It's logical, she thought, that Debbie was reaching out for her father, whom she loved, in her last desperate moments.

Jane Kline took Dorothy into Debbie's bedroom, letting the psychic feel articles of Debbie's clothing. Dorothy saw the shiny high-school ring and put it on her finger.

"Let me wear this for a while," she asked the mother. "I feel it will bring me luck."

Handling beloved possessions of victims often triggered strong impressions for the psychic. As with Doreen Carlucci's bracelet, Dorothy often found that these articles helped her feel sure she was on the right track. If an object did not seem to fit her feelings about a person, then she would question the veracity of those feelings or the genuineness of the article. She felt many times, too, that the auras of personal articles brought her luck, as she had said to Jane Kline. In this instance luck meant being certain that Debbie Kline was the person she had in focus.

As soon as Dorothy had the ring, she felt that its owner no longer lived. She knew that Debbie Kline was dead.

Paul Weachter, a young, dark, curly haired state trooper in his late thirties, waited with the family as Dorothy prepared herself psychically and physically for the day's hunt. Weachter had not worked on the Kline case before but had been assigned to work with the psychic over the weekend, since the trooper who had been working on the case was on vacation. Bright and energetic, Weachter was willing to try anything Dorothy requested. Along with the two newspaper reporters and Dorothy's family, he helped her interpret clues.

Others, however, were not as willing to acquiesce to her visions. Sergeant Hussack, Weachter's superior, let it be known that he was not in accord with the psychic's investigatory procedures. What Dorothy did not yet know was that her presence, in less than one week, was to stir a wide wave of public skepticism.

While everyone stood in the Kline's living room, where pictures of children and grandchildren were placed all around, Dorothy pulled out a set of long underwear and went into Debbie and her sister's room for a quick change. She was not going to take any chance of getting frostbite on this bleak January day.

The Kline children stood silently as Dorothy reappeared, her short, solid body wrapped in a bright ski parka and black knitted pants, and a colorfully woven ski cap pulled over her forehead. She smiled and motioned her arm as if leading troops forward. Trooper Weachter followed Dorothy to his car, where Bob, Paul Allison, and the two reporters joined them. A second car, containing friends of Dick Kline, followed close behind. This group was openly skeptical, questioning Dorothy's moves and vision at every turn. It seemed as though a sports event were about to begin.

Dorothy's first instinct was to head for a dumping ground in the area. She tried to describe to Paul Weachter how she envisioned the dump, but any site would be difficult to recognize under two or more feet of snow. Following her instructions, the officer drove to a hill where a small dumping area was located. Rather than point to the ground, though, Dorothy indicated a house at the bottom of the hill, which she felt was important to Debbie. It was the home of Debbie's former boyfriend.

One of the group who had come in the second car was Eldon Joiner. He asked Dorothy why she couldn't just tell the police where to go and find the girl. Dorothy explained that her psychic sense did not work that way.

"I have to proceed at a pace that takes me closer and closer to feelings I can identify within me. When something is right, I know it," she told the Southerner. "I know this girl is dead." Eldon blanched at the psychic's brutal pronouncement.

"Surely you don't just see that?" he wondered in amazement.

"I do just see that. If she was in water, I could tell you where she is and what time we'd find her. But she didn't drown. So, if you want to follow us around, you better keep quiet and quit complaining."

Joiner admired Dorothy's confidence, even if he didn't particularly like her tongue.

Dorothy repeated to Weachter and Joiner her older statement to Jane Kline, that she saw an outside oven somewhere, and something "burnt."

"Burnt?" Joiner asked.

"No, I see the word "burnt," not necessarily something burned."

The men were confounded. "What kind of oven?" Weachter asked.

"I don't think it's still used. What's more important," Dorothy went on, "is the yellow I keep seeing. We have to find all that yellow. I saw it the first time I spoke with Jane Kline. We'll find her just beyond that yellow. Her body is near a blue swimming pool. That's what we should be looking for."

Joiner looked at the state trooper and shrugged.

When they arrived at another field surrounded by dense trees on the outskirts of the town, Dorothy began to get a picture of the man she felt had murdered Debbie Kline. Paul Weachter was walking next to her. She told him that the man she saw had straight, thinning hair worn combed to one side. He was about five feet eight, but she reminded Weachter that height was not her best dimension.

"He's thin, maybe no more than a hundred forty pounds. I see him with someone who looks to me like an animal." And she made a face of disgust.

"Wait, I feel you should know something about one of these men," Dorothy suddenly said. "Yes, one is known by the police now. I think he recently tried to rape someone, but she managed to stop him. Something went wrong. The police somewhere in the area know him," she said confidently.

Dorothy kept walking slowly, her short legs kicking up puffs of snow as she tried to focus on the man she saw in a prison cell. Once again she stopped. "I'm beginning to see this beast. This man doesn't deserve to be alive."

Weachter immediately showed Dorothy pictures of suspects that he was carrying in his car. Dorothy flipped through the stack quickly, stopping once and handing the selected photograph to the officer.

"This is him. If his name is Robert, Richard, or Ronald, you've got number one."

"You're sure there were two . . . ," he started.

"I see what I see. I know there were two men," she insisted, "and neither of them had ever seen Debbie Kline before that day. It's the other animal that has the double letters in his last name. God protect us from people like this. This guy"—pointing to the picture Weachter held— "will lead us to the other bastard. You're not going to want to see what these guys did to that girl."

Weachter felt chilled and excited by what he sensed Dorothy was seeing. The photo he held was of a man he knew was sitting in jail. His name was Richard Lee Dodson, a thirty-year-old from nearby Greencastle. He wondered if Dorothy knew this man was being held in the Franklin County Prison on a charge of attempted rape of a twenty-six-year-old housewife in Fort McCord.

Richard Lee Dodson, as Dorothy had sensed, was not a neophyte criminal. His dealings with the Franklin County juvenile authorities had begun at the age of thirteen in 1959, and his dalliance with the authorities had continued through a series of altercations, until 1972, when twenty-six-year-old Dodson, then married with four children, was picked up for raping a fourteen-year-old girl. The rape charge was dismissed in plea bargaining, leaving him guilty of indecent-liberties charges.

Then, two days before his sentencing, Dodson's house had mysteriously burned to the ground, killing his wife and three of his children. His still-breathing four-year-old son was severely burned and permanently institutionalized in a burn clinic. People thought it odd that Dodson had been home at the time but had escaped unscathed.

He was, in any case, sentenced to four to six years in the Illinois Correctional Institute. Later he was transferred to Vienna Prison, where his cellmate was Ronald Henninger.

Henninger's record made the justice system look like a hunk of Swiss cheese. Henninger had eight AWOL counts against him before his dismissal from the navy; later he accrued up to eighteen years of prison tenancy, though paroles were twice awarded him.

After his second parole in February, 1973, he was charged with fleeing police, aggravated assault, several motor-vehicle violations, and murder. The violations were part of an attempted escape from a rifle-shooting incident, in which Henninger killed Francis "Frank" Fenton, a murder which he had been hired to commit. After two trials Henninger pleaded guilty to involuntary manslaughter and was sentenced to three to ten years in Joliet Prison. In 1975, he was transferred to Vienna Prison, and paroled on April Fool's Day, 1976.

Henninger's daughter, Lorrie, who at the age of five had been shipped off to a foster home with her two other siblings, found her father in Vienna Prison after years of not knowing anything about him. Lorrie, then eighteen and beautiful, was introduced by her father to his cellmate, Richard Dodson, with whom she fell in love. Dodson's parole, on May 26, 1976, was partly arranged by Henninger's claiming him as a relative. Lorrie and Richard were married shortly after his parole, when he was full of promises and new horizons.

In December, Dodson took a job with a local oil delivery company. It was while making the rounds through a

Fort McCord neighborhood that he stopped at a house under the pretense of delivering oil on a cold winter day and attacked the attractive woman who answered the door. The rape was thwarted, however, by the woman's resistance. Dodson left, warning her he would be back to finish the job.

It was Trooper Paul Weachter who had been summoned to the Fort McCord woman's home. She identified Dodson, and Weachter persuaded her to testify against him in court. Leaving the quiet residential home, Weachter noticed an oil truck passing through the street, slowing down in front of the house he had just left.

He stopped the truck and found that the driver fit the description the woman had given. It was Dodson, coming back for more. That afternoon he was charged, without bail, with attempted rape. That was on January 13—the day Dorothy had predicted to Jane Kline as a significant date.

Weachter led Dorothy and the psychic posse back to his car, telling her that he was planning to go to the jail later. After hours of searching, Joiner and his friends also decided to return to their warm houses. Dorothy was glad to see the skeptics leave her in peace. However, after years of working with police, she preferred honest skeptics like Eldon Joiner to people who pretended to trust her. She knew she would have him convinced by the end of that week.

All the hours that Dorothy trudged through the snow, following her psychic instincts, the townspeople were listening to radio reports of her arrival, each station promising to be the first to get news of Debbie Kline's discovery. Believers and skeptics alike listened from their homes, from the hospital, the jail, and businesses. A small contingent of nonbelievers had voiced their opinion that the psychic was a "devil woman," and soon their views developed into a small controversy carried over into the local newspapers.

As Appolonia had told her, it was God who gave Dorothy the gift of vision, and she had never doubted that. God worked in odd ways, allowing so many children to see so much tragedy. But Dorothy knew it wasn't God who took those children; it was human ignorance and perversity that destroyed lives, and she only wanted to help the victims safely on their way to God's protection.

As Dorothy had matured, with the help of believers, practice, and hypnosis, she had begun to see that her life had taken on a special meaning. She felt she was a messenger of St. Anthony, whose image never left her. She would spend her time helping the totally helpless and innocent, especially children. No one, Dorothy felt, spent enough time worrying and caring for children.

In fact she believed that those people claiming she was a "devil woman" could spend their time better by communicating with their children and families. She was deeply saddened by this undercurrent of bigotry, realizing its potential power.

But at the moment Dorothy was more concerned with a new mental picture she was getting—a vision of trouble at the jail.

"Someone is going to try and break. Warn the guards," she told Weachter. "Today is very dangerous for a policeman. Someone at the jail had better be careful. I get the feeling of being unable to breathe. It's funny, it's not like being buried or underground or something like that . . . just unable to breathe. It's like being smothered."

Cox and Peiffer took down the words verbatim. Weachter absorbed the information, not knowing what to do with it.

As it happened, a jailbreak was attempted at the Franklin County Detention Center at 4:50 P.M., just three hours and twenty minutes later. A sixteen-year-old inmate grabbed a matron and tried to choke her to death in order to secure her keys. As it was reported on the front page of the next day's paper, another guard, overhearing the scuffle, rescued her, breaking the grip of the boy's hands on her neck, thus thwarting the escape attempt.

Weachter, in the meantime, made certain that all the inmates of Franklin County Prison heard the news of the visiting psychic on the radio. And the next day the young state officer, having heard of the predicted escape attempt coming to pass, would go beyond the call of duty. He went to visit Richard Lee Dodson.

Weachter met with Dodson in a small, windowless room while a guard stood at the door. Dodson was nervous, his cocksure attitude having diminished in the past week. The Kline case, after so many months of dormancy, seemed to be boiling again. On the table Weachter had placed various newspaper articles Dorothy had given him which covered some of her previous cases. Weachter asked Dodson to leaf through the material. The officer was not going to use any other force than logic.

"I've spent the last two days working with this woman," he said to the prisoner, pointing to a picture of Dorothy and her dog Jason. "Do you believe in psychics, Dodson?" he asked.

"Guess so," he shrugged. "They say she's a devil woman."

"Maybe so," Weachter said. "She's got me convinced, though. She told us there was going to be a break yesterday in the jail. Did you hear that?"

Dodson nodded. "Yeah, they've been buzzing it up all morning."

Weachter was glad everyone had heard about Dorothy's prediction coming true. Next he took a stack of photos from his briefcase and held them before the accused rapist.

"I handed these to Mrs. Allison yesterday. She looked through them and picked out one picture." He let the photo of Dodson drop to the table. "She handed me this picture and said, 'If his name is Richard, Robert, or Ronald, you've got your man!'" Weachter stared directly into Dodson's eyes. "Do you have anything to say?"

Dodson looked away.

"She also said that Debbie Kline's body was next to a blue swimming pool. Does that mean anything to you?"

Dodson said nothing.

"She also said there were two of you and that both of you had been involved in rape before, and that now you hated each other. Well, what do you have to say?" Weachter pursued.

"Nothing, damn it. I never met the woman before." His voice sounded angry. "She's no cop. She can't accuse me of a thing."

"Right. She can't, but we can. You just think about it for a while and anytime you want to talk, just let the guard know. I'll listen anytime."

Weachter got up, picked up the scattered papers, and left the prisoner staring at the blank wall.

Dodson sat in his prison cell, the world slipping away from him. Anger permeated his thoughts as his chances for freedom grew dimmer.

Henninger, his mentor, was in prison in Illinois, but Dodson had learned from his wife that Henninger intended to return to Pennsylvania and finish him off.

Dodson might have wondered how it could be that he had managed to dance with the law for so many years, winning so much of the time, only to be hounded by a devil woman. He must have reflected on that drunken summer afternoon in July when he and Henninger had picked out Debbie Kline coming out of the hospital, and how Henninger had decided to show Dodson "how to really pick up a woman with ease." And how Henninger had slit her throat after they had both had sex with her, and how she had stood silent before them, as if defying them in death. Whatever his thoughts, Dorothy was zeroing in on him quickly, and so, too, were the police.

At the Kline house Jane and Dick wondered what kind of success this psychic would have. Would this woman find their daughter? Could she, in two days, do what dozens had been unable to do in six months? Was it worth being hopeful, only to be disappointed again?

Before Dorothy left for the hotel with her husband and son, Jane cornered her in Debbie's room.

"Mrs. Allison, I just want to know the truth," Jane said in her nasal, Southern accent. "Please, I beg you, tell me the truth. Is my daughter still alive? Do you see her living?" the poor mother struggled.

For the first time, Dorothy was going to break one of her cardinal rules.

"No," Dorothy said, taking the woman's hand into her own. "I'm afraid I don't. All I can tell you is that in my vision I feel she died quickly, not long after you missed her."

The grieving mother sat on the bed and wept.

Before Dorothy left on Sunday evening, she told Weachter and the two reporters that they should keep "doubles" in mind. The area in which Debbie would be found had double letters in it; the incidents she predicted might happen twice; and the murderers, of which there were two, had performed such crimes twice before.

She told Dick Kline that she sensed this was the second murder in his family, that he had had a close relative killed not too far from where Debbie was taken. Surprised, Dick corroborated the fact that his uncle had been mysteriously murdered only seven years before in the general area in which Debbie had disappeared.

Before she drove back to Nutley with Bob and Paul, the tired and cold psychic told Weachter that Debbie had not been buried. She would be found on a high spot from which great expanses could be seen and that she would be on some sort of "line." Again, she was bothered by a large plastic sheet that she was beginning to think might be the swimming pool.

"Look in two directions," she told him. "If we've been looking south, then head north tomorrow and see if any of the clues fit."

She also promised to undergo hypnosis with Dr. Ribner on the following Friday. At that time she would "get in the car with Debbie" and drive the last miles with her.

"Hopefully, I'll never make it to Ribner's," she said, hugging everyone good-bye. "I think you're going to find Debbie this week. Before Friday."

Monday's *Record Herald* headlines were about Dorothy's prediction of the attempted break and her prophecy that Debbie Kline would be found within days. A photo was run of Dorothy holding a Princeton T-shirt, which had been given her by the Hearsts. It had belonged to their daughter, Patty. The article accompanying the photo described the psychic's more famous involvements.

Richard Dodson read the papers and thought about

132

Weachter's words and Dorothy's visions. That afternoon he told the guard to have word sent to Weachter that he had something to say to the officer.

On Tuesday evening Dorothy spoke with reporter Bob Cox about further feelings she was getting from her home regarding the case. She told him that she felt something "drastic" would happen in the area within six hours. As the reporter told it in the paper, she said, "I see a brick building. Watch the corners. There could be a knifing. The building looks like the one I saw before."

As before, Dorothy's prediction was accurate.

"At 10:45 P.M. a second assault on a matron at Franklin County Detention Center was made by an inmate," Cox wrote. "It came less than four hours after the telephone call."

Again Dorothy had foreseen an event at the jail in which Richard Dodson was being held. She was focusing so acutely on the prisoner that she was picking up other prisoners' vibrations. Weachter was excited by the news.

It was on Wednesday morning that Paul Weachter and three other officials drove with Richard Dodson to the point where he claimed he could find Debbie Kline's body. Heading north over the double low bridges on Route 16, they drove fifty-one miles toward the Franklin-Huntington county lines. As they approached the mountainous area where the body was supposedly located, they passed a barrage of yellow warning signs and then, a large yellow billboard advertising rooms at "Burnt Cabins," a small resort area.

Dodson pointed them to an area high on the mountainside that commanded a view of the valleys. This was where they had taken the quiet, frightened girl that summer day and shattered her life. Now, snow covered everything.

They parked the car and walked toward a pile of rubble. One of the policemen picked up a blue plastic swimming pool that was on top of a pile and saw a white shoe and part of a leg sticking out.

The body, essentially a skeleton now, was dressed in a white pants suit and white shoes. The remains could not be readily identified as male or female, and the autopsy would have to be delayed until the body had thawed. Cumberland

County Coroner Dr. Robert J. McConanghie eventually attributed death to hemorrhaging from a neck wound.

"It's hard to pinpoint," he said. "When you don't have skin or tissue or a windpipe to work with. There was evidence of blood around the neck."

Using teeth, chest X-rays, hair, and clothing found on the corpse, the police were able to identify the body as Deborah Sue Kline's.

News spread quickly in the quiet communities that the psychic's predictions had come to pass. Dorothy was in Florida working on the other case she had taken on when she heard that Debbie had been found. She had several other cases demanding her help, so the success of the Kline case gave her a new boost of energy.

A confession to kidnapping and rape came from Richard Dodson the following day. At the same time he named Ronald Henninger as Debbie's murderer. As Dorothy had foreseen, plenty of doubles were involved, including double rapist-murderers.

After Debbie's burial, the community continued its tug-of-war over the use of the psychic. Different religious groups had their own reasons for either not wanting her to be credited or wanting her to receive proper reward for her work. In an interview in the *Public Opinion*, Sergeant Hussack said he was not one to join the bandwagon of accolades.

"To the best of my knowledge," he told reporter Marie Lanser, "she hasn't helped us. We weren't pursuing her predictions—we weren't relying on Mrs. Allison."

The following Wednesday's edition ran two letters from irate citizens, shaking an angry finger at Hussack, under the headline of "State Police Said Unfair to Mrs. Allison." Both letters were from Chambersburg residents who did not know the Klines personally. One said "Give credit where it is due—to Mrs. Allison. May God bless Mrs. Allison as she continues the fine work she does of helping police find missing children."

In pointing out that Sergeant Hussack was "downplaying Mrs. Allison's role," the same writer enumerated all the details given by the psychic and the consequent discoveries. Dorothy had a strong support base.

But was God on her side? In this religious community it was a controversial question.

As far as the Klines were concerned, God was a topic better left alone. Jane Kline declined to discuss the subject. For months she had placed Debbie's picture on her white Bible, always left open on the mantel. Everyday the desperate mother took hold of the Book and prayed. She read till she could feel no more.

Richard Kline said, "This kind of thing makes us wonder. Something like this happens and you don't know which way to turn. Feels like a fence walker: either side looks wrong."

Both of the Klines credited Dorothy with being the strongest influence in locating their daughter. One of the local Methodist ministers, however, took exception. In an article entitled "Psychics Forbidden in Biblical Times," Reverend Glen A. Miller of Greencastle saw the psychic's involvement as an omen of universal bad times.

After thanking the Lord for returning Debbie's body, he went on to say "that it is recorded in I Samuel 28" where "Saul wanted to hear from God. He sought answers in the appointed ways and God refused to give answers. His refusal came because of wickedness and disobedience in the government." So Saul sought a medium.

The minister emphasized that psychics are forbidden in other parts of the scriptures, as well. "It is a sad commentary on the spiritual level of our nation when psychics are called upon to give answers."

And yet another prominently placed argument was run by a concerned pastor from State Line, Pennsylvania. Pastor Fisler of Trinity United Brethren Church wrote that the *Record Herald* had given "extensive coverage to Dorothy Allison and her role," overlooking the "community prayer service held at the Antrim Faith Baptist Church on January 6, 1977."

Reminding the readers that "God can still perform miracles" and that "if you want an amazing turn of events, consider the stated purpose of that January 6 prayer service and what actually happened last week when the suspect from the Franklin County Detention Center stepped forth to show authorities where Debbie's body was buried.

"It seems to me that prayer was answered explicitly. It would be good to see headlines that say 'God Answered Prayer' instead of continual headlines telling about a psychic's predictions."

Dorothy was irritated by all the religious hooplah. It was her being called a devil woman that had triggered fear in the incarcerated suspect, however. She felt that perhaps, in this case, being partnered with the "devil" was a godsend.

The Washington Township Police made Dorothy an honorary member of the department and presented her with a badge.

In February stories about Dorothy began to appear over the AP wires across America, in police journals, and in the *Star* and *National Enquirer*. Each month she would receive hundreds of letters begging for her help. All the letters were handled by Lubertazzi and his wife. Many of the letters would be from spouses whose "better halves" had absconded with their children. "I know they've got to be in the Pittsburgh area," the plea would say, "couldn't you help me find them? Look at these faces, wouldn't you miss them too?"

Chapter 6

When Kathy Hennessy woke up on March 5, 1977, the Saturday morning before her birthday, she was full of expectation and excitement. The next day she would have her party. The brown-eyed child with long brown hair decided, as she sat atop her bed, that she would make a list on her typewriter of presents she wanted, and she would include a present for her brother.

The house was quiet. Her five year old brother, Spanky, was still sleeping. Carol, her mother, was at the Deborah Heart and Lung Center in Brown Mills, where she worked as a nurse's aide. Kathy's tall, lean father, Sergeant John Hennessy, was sound asleep after working the night shift at McGuire Air Force Base. Kathy knew better than to make too much noise, averting the ire of her sleeping father, who wouldn't awaken till sometime late in the afternoon.

Kathy was a precocious, lively seven-year-old, who had a reputation for being intelligent and brave. One neighbor recalled the summer before when she was bitten on the leg by a dog.

"Blood gushed out, but Kathy was very calm," the friend said. "I drove her to the hospital because her mother was at work, and doctors had to stitch the wound.

"But Kathy was able to tell us her daddy's telephone

number where he worked at McGuire AFB, as well as her mother's number. Even the nurse said how brave she was. The only question asked was if she was going to lose her leg," the neighbor reported.

Quietly the slender girl slipped into the den with her child-sized typewriter. She put the machine on a small table in front of the television and proceeded to write a story about a girl friend who had angered her the day before. At the same time she watched cartoons and waited for her brother to awaken so they could go to the park and play.

That Saturday was special for many residents of Pemberton Township. The weather gave people reason to believe that winter was on the wane. The skies cleared, and clouds gave way to a radiating sun. Some thirty miles south of Trenton, New Jersey's capital, Pemberton Township can be a bleak spot in winter, located as it is on the perimeter of New Jersey's rural pine barrens, an area dotted with lakes and streams and mostly sandy soil.

Locals welcomed the warm day that allowed them to escape the monotony and bleakness of the military-base architecture that dominates the pre-Revolutionary town. McGuire Air Force Base and adjoining Fort Dix are the largest employers in the area, seconded only by berry farming and picking, which accounts for a sizeable migrant-worker influx each year.

But by the end of that sunny afternoon grim newspaper headlines in the *Burlington County Times* all but banished the day's pleasures: "Br. Mills girl killed, dumped in lake."

Two women, a nursing student and her fiancé's teen-age sister, had been out walking that afternoon around the lake known as Lake-in-the-Woods and frequently referred to as Hidden Lake. In a wooded area sometimes used as a picnic site, the lake was located just below a hill known by winter sledders as Suicide Hill. While enjoying the day, the two women discovered the body of a little girl floating face-down in the shallow waters of a trickling rill.

The pair ran to their nearby home in the Brown Mills section of Pemberton and phoned the police. The two women and the fiancé's mother ran back to the site to see if any aid could help the child and to wait for the arrival of the police.

Because the body was found six hundred feet out of the township and on Fort Dix property, the investigation was spearheaded by the Federal Bureau of Investigation, and assisted by nonfederal forces. The federal agents in charge of the investigation came from the Fort Dix military police, the Criminal Investigation Division (CID) of Fort Dix, and the office of Security Investigation at McGuire Air Force Base. The nonfederal forces were headed by the Pemberton Township Police Department with support from the Burlington County prosecutor's office, and the New Jersey State Police.

The unidentified body was a grim sight. When Dr. Arthur Webber arrived from his post at Walson Army Hospital, he found "the body had no heartbeat or pulsebeats . . . it was cold and pale." He pronounced the child dead.

The little girl was naked from the waist down, and her red-and-blue checked sweater was pushed up beneath her arms. Blue shorts were found ten feet away from the body, turned inside out, the zipper down and broken. A pair of underpants, also inside out, were caught on a twig in the water. Bruises and cuts covered the child's face and body.

The corpse was removed and taken to the army hospital where an autopsy would be performed that night by Dr. Joseph DiLorenzo, the Burlington County Medical examiner.

The Fort Dix team heading the investigation at the site of the child's demise had no forensic pathological experience; hence, when Lieutenant Detective Richard Serafin, the Pemberton policeman heading the casework, arrived on the scene, he had no chance to look for clues as the body had been removed and the evidence improperly marked. The crime scene was contaminated.

News of the murder spread and consumed the community with instant terror and fear. Word of a slain child channeled through the massive military post and throughout the town. For several hours the local radio blared news of the death, trying to identify the lost child.

Helicopters buzzed like hungry vultures over the wooded area, looking for any clues that would lead to the

139

girl's murderer. Federal agents scoured the vicinity while bloodhounds clawed their way through the underbrush. Both on and off the post, agents and police began the long, arduous task of interviewing anyone and everyone who might have been in the area that bright sunny day when Kathy Hennessy was raped and murdered less than half a mile from her home.

When Carol Hennessy returned home from work around 6:30 P.M., she saw Spanky playing listlessly in the yard. When she inquired as to his sister's whereabouts, the little boy shrugged his shoulders.

A next-door neighbor came running over to see if Kathy was home. She told Carol that she had heard news reports that a little girl's body had been found nearby that afternoon.

Carol ran into the house, searching and yelling for her child. John Hennessy asked her what the urgency was about, and Carol told him about the radio reports.

Within minutes Carol and John were on their way to the hospital to see if their child was the victim being reported.

The post mortem results from Dr. DiLorenzo painted a gruesome, frightening picture of Kathy's last living moments. The time of death was placed between 1:00 and 2:00 P.M. Suffocation was given as the cause of death, possibly by a hand held over her mouth and nostrils.

Dr. DiLorenzo told authorities, "There is no doubt there was a physical attack and that it was violent." The fact that the child had been sodomized was not publicly reported, nor was the fact that seminal fluid was found in her mouth.

More details magnified the horror. She had twenty-one lacerations of her face and body, fourteen black and blue marks beneath the skin—"probably from punches," Dr. DiLorenzo hypothesized—plus four abrasions or scrape marks.

"Her skull," the doctor added, "had five separate bruises inflicted by punches."

He went on to conjecture that "considerable force was used by either a punch or a good shot from the knee," as most of the contusions were on the child's belly and pelvic area.

In trying to remove the child's shorts, the rapist-murderer left several deep trenches in her inner thighs.

As Kathy's school picture ran on the front page of all the local papers, and as the hunt for the person who could murder a seven-year-old ensued, the town tightened its hatches. An aura of tension and fear pervaded the vicinity. Each media report stoked the flames of fear. This was especially true since reports from the autopsy were leaked; most details had been kept from the media.

Lieutenant Serafin had his hands full. The fact that the murder was a rape, and a brutal one, acted like a powerful fuel, igniting paronoia in mothers, fathers, and teachers, all of whom suddenly took hysterical precautions with their children. Every reason anyone could find to be suspicious of his fellow man, whether neighbor or stranger, was apparent in the atmosphere. Wild reports of child molestations began to filter in at an increasing rate. The very air of the town seemed an incubator for fabricated stories.

Several days into the investigation, Detective Bud Fifield was investigating an attempted abduction report. He approached a ten-year-old girl and asked if her mother was home.

"The kid went bananas," Fifield reported. "She started screaming, 'Don't hurt me, please don't hurt me.'"

Lieutenant Serafin cited the case of a Fort Dix six-year-old who had returned home from school and told her adult baby-sitter that she had seen a man pulling a little girl into the woods.

"She described the man and his victim right down to the color of their clothes," the stout, blond lieutenant said.

Nearly seventy-five agents, military police, and local and state police officers moved with lightning speed to the described area. Helicopters and hounds were brought in, as well.

"We became suspicious when she told us the victim was wearing a coat," Serafin said. "The weather was hot that day. Too hot for the heavy coat this kid described."

After two hours of searching, the child admitted to having made up the whole story, "to see what would happen."

* * *

In an attempt to piece together Kathy's last hours, an appeal was made to any children or adults who might possess information about Kathy's actions between noon Saturday and 2:00 P.M. to call a special telephone number at Fort Dix.

One report came in from a fourteen-year-old ninth grader from Pemberton Township High School. He and his father had been motorbike-riding that day in the area where the second grader's body was found. The father, a master sergeant at McGuire, confirmed that they had seen a girl "standing with a man with gray hair next to a light brown pickup truck." Since the pair looked like a father and daughter loading firewood into the truck, neither sensed anything odd about the sight.

"A half hour later the truck drove off," the father said. "I don't know if anyone was in the vehicle with the driver."

Upward of eighty men, mostly federal agents, made every effort to track down the man and the truck. Other calls led to a search for another man said to have been seen near the crime scene. Described as white, between forty and fifty years of age, the man was seen driving an old white car, probably a Ford.

The FBI stressed the point that these people were not necessarily suspects, they were merely being sought for information.

One unanswerable question was why Kathy had not been with her brother, Spanky. An FBI agent had interrogated the five-year-old twice and was unable to ascertain whether or not the boy had been with his sister. Spanky said he had been playing in the nearby park, but when the agent asked more specific questions, the boy answered in non sequiturs.

Rumors abounded throughout the area that an AWOL recruit was being sought as chief suspect. Another widely accepted notion was that the murderer was a teen-aged boy.

"There's so much pot smoking and narcotics around here," one woman neighbor railed.

In the meantime Detective Serafin worked with the FBI

in accumulating from their files every known sex offender within a fifty-mile radius.

"This is a crude area," the detective said. "It's a melting pot of problems. Incest is prevalent here. Parent problems lead to juvenile delinquency problems."

In 1975, the Pemberton Police Department had instituted a Juvenile Bureau, with two men working full time with children and teen-agers. Since the beginning of the project, over two hundred fifty cases of child abuse had been reported. For a small area with a population of fifty thousand, the figure was high.

Five days after the battered body of Kathy Hennessy was found, she was buried in an out-of-state military cemetery, following funeral services in a Brown Mills mortuary. John Hennessy, wanting to avoid any carnival atmosphere, insisted upon private services.

The young parents, both in their late twenties, had been preparing to leave New Jersey, as the sergeant's time with the Air Force would terminate in May. Kathy was buried in North Carolina where her parents were from and where they would follow her some time that summer.

John and Carol Hennessy had declined to talk with reporters while they endured the shock and horror of their daughter's death. A reward was posted for $5,000 to anyone offering information which would lead to the arrest and conviction of the murderer. The reward came from the hospital foundation of the famed Deborah Heart and Lung Center where Carol was employed.

"This reward is offered by Deborah as an expression of a sense of responsibility to the community of Browns Mills and its staff of more than four hundred employees," hospital president Rubin E. Cohen said.

The relentless search continued. Hundreds of persons were interviewed, both police and federal agents going door to door to speak to anyone and everyone. Through constant checking, the man and girl who were reported seen near the crime site were found.

"He's clean," one investigator reported. "We've talked to him and the girl, and checked them with others on the scene. They were collecting wood for their fireplace."

143

The man and girl, however, gave investigators leads to others who were on the scene that Saturday afternoon. The search for the fortyish Caucasian was redoubled, and two younger men were sought as possible suspects. Two other young women who had been in the woods that day described a nineteen or twenty-year-old man who had been near the wooded area.

"He was standing at the side of the road, looking down at his hands," one of the women said. "He turned and looked at us for about thirty seconds, and then he took off into the woods."

The woman described the mystery man as about five feet seven inches tall, of average build, with shoulder-length fuzzy blond hair and wearing blue jeans and a blue-plaid flannel shirt.

Another young man reported in the area was described as sporting a Christlike beard and longish, medium-brown hair. The second man was also in his late teens, of slim build, and was said to be wearing an army jacket with the number "19" over the breast pocket.

These descriptions were conveyed to an artist from the New Jersey State Police, and a composite drawing was made of each of the two men.

The composites were drawn by New Jersey State Patrolman George Homa. Serafin had called in the Trenton-born patrolman whose reputation as a freehand composite artist had spread around the country.

Most composite artists, those people who wallpaper the world with mug shots and criminal likenesses, use a special kit equipped with plastic overlays fitting any facial feature that exists in stock shapes and sizes. Homa's natural gift allows him to draw freehand and interpret the witnesses' mental picture with incredible precision, even if the perception is based on a thirty-second glance.

The FBI released the composites to news media on March 10, hoping the public would lead them to the men. The artist's rendering of the man with the Christlike beard was identified as David Geary, who immediately became a prime suspect.

The number of investigators working on the case grew to over one hundred, culled from the various units involved.

144

Special Agent Louis Giovanetti, in charge of the FBI in New Jersey, termed it a "major investigation."

All around, investigators were frustrated. A rape and murder that occurred in the middle of the day when people were out and enjoying the sun had to have been seen by someone. Detective Jim Buck, one of Serafin's men, decided that if no one locally reported seeing the murderer, maybe a psychic could help. He had just read a magazine article about a psychic in Nutley. The magazine, *New Jersey's Finest*, was a Patrolman's Benevolent Association publication. The article chronicled the Debbie Kline case and others that Dorothy Allison had helped resolve in the last ten years.

Buck entered Serafin's office the morning of March 11, with coffee in hand, to discuss progress on the Hennessy case. It was at that time that he asked his superior if he'd ever worked with a psychic.

"You nuts?" the detective exclaimed.

"We've tried everything else," Jim Buck started.

"Bullshit. We've got enough problems. I could just see the FBI's face if I told them we were talking to a psychic."

Buck pursued the topic by mentioning the article he had read. In his fifteen years with the department Serafin had never heard of using a psychic. However, the fact that the patrolman's magazine had written about a psychic detective piqued his interest.

"I've never worked with a psychic. I have no idea how valid they are," Serafin admitted. He thought to himself that the weight of the investigation was on the FBI, not on him. He was in a good position to try different avenues of investigation, if he saw fit, without reporting it to the FBI.

That night Serafin took the magazine home and read about the Nutley psychic who had helped police and FBI from San Francisco, in the Patty Hearst case, to Munich, Germany. In the article a policeman from the Nutley police department, Salvatore Lubertazzi, was interviewed. Serafin decided he would call the detective in Nutley the next morning.

Richard Serafin, born of Polish and English parents, was raised in the area around Pemberton Township. In his mid-thirties, Serafin enjoyed his position in the department of forty-two men, the largest police department in the county.

"In a small department," he explains, "I've had experience with everything from family squabbles to homicides. The big-city cops are pigeonholed and seldom get beyond their specialties."

Serafin's father was a strict disciplinarian. Serafin feels this has given him an insight into military homelife, where the father's ideas of discipline and the children's world of peer pressures and change constantly clash. Through a hard-nosed skeptic in many situations, he has learned to judge quietly, giving him an amiable way of dealing with humanity.

In calling Nutley, the dubious detective decided to give as little information as possible. He simply told Lupo that "we have a murder case down here I'd like to discuss with Mrs. Allison." He said nothing about the age or sex of the victim.

Lupo told him he would call Dorothy and ask her if she had time to work on another case. The Nutley detective told Serafin that she was working on several cases at the moment, that hundreds of letters requesting her attention were piled on his desk, and that he had to let her use her feelings as a guide to choosing.

"Either way," Lupo said, "someone will call you back and let you know."

Serafin put the phone down, noticing his palms were moist from nervousness. He didn't expect to hear from the psychic or Lupo. Serafin's feeling was that psychics, like astrologers, gave such general information that they could describe the world in a universal adjective.

The detective was surprised when Detective Lubertazzi called fifteen minutes later.

"She says she would be glad to help you," Lubertazzi said, his own voice sounding surprised. "Right away she sensed something. I don't know if this is going to mean anything to you, but she sees running water and brown uniforms."

"How in hell can she see anything when she doesn't know a thing about the case?" Serafin asked. He figured

Lubertazzi must have read something about the case in the papers and must have coached the psychic. Then again, Serafin thought, not much publicity had seeped to other parts of New Jersey.

Lupo gave Dorothy's telephone number to Serafin and also told Serafin to call him anytime he needed an explanation of how Dorothy went about her investigations.

"You ever worked with a psychic before?" Lupo asked.

"Nope. Can't say I have," Serafin answered.

Lupo laughed to himself, making Serafin wonder what he was getting himself into.

"Tighten your seat belt," Lupo warned, "you're in for a psychic roller coaster." And he hung up.

Serafin decided Lubertazzi had to be on the psychic's payroll. He imagined the prices she charged were steep. But curiosity had gotten the better of him, and he decided he would pursue the woman.

He put a fresh cassette into his recording machine and dialed Dorothy's number. He told the pleasant-sounding woman that he had never worked with a psychic before, and that he had said "bullshit" to the detective who had suggested calling in a psychic. He also told her that if it were okay with her, he would record their conversations. Dorothy consented.

"I'll ask the questions," Serafin said. "If you're right about something, I'll tell you."

"That's fine with me," Dorothy said. "Did Lubertazzi tell you that I got something right away? Did he tell you about the running water and brown uniforms? Do they mean anything to you?"

"Running water and brown uniforms?" the detective repeated. "I guess they do mean something. Our victim was found in water and on Fort Dix property. There are lots of brown uniforms around."

"I don't get the little girl drowning," Dorothy thought out loud.

"How did you know it was a little girl?" Serafin snapped.

"I saw that from the beginning. That's why I told Lupo I would talk to you. I felt it was a child, and hearing your voice I got it was a little girl. *That's* how," Dorothy responded in kind to the nervous detective. "Also, you told Lupo it was a murder."

"A pure murder?" Serafin tested her.

"I don't think so. Let me think," Dorothy said and honed in on her feelings about the little girl, who was slowly evolving in her focus. "Dear God," Dorothy exclaimed. "The little thing has been sexually assaulted. Oh, that poor child and those poor parents. Do they know?"

"Yes," Serafin said, "they know everything."

"That she was raped vaginally, orally, and anally?" Dorothy moaned.

Serafin was shocked by what he heard. He could not believe that this woman had given him information that had not been disclosed to the media. Only those closest to the investigation knew that Kathy Hennessy had been sodomized.

"Mrs. Allison, did you read about this case anywhere?" Serafin inquired.

"How could I read about it? You're in another part of the world, for all I know."

Serafin was excited and confused. He wanted to end the conversation and think. "Do you see anything else?" he asked.

"Yes. I think the person who did it was young, and he has an alcohol problem," Dorothy offered. "Do you have the girl's date of birth?" she asked.

"No, not right here. I'll get it for you and call you again tomorrow. Okay?" the anxious caller said.

"Fine with me. I should be home most of the day." And she hung up.

Serafin turned off the recording machine and lit a cigarette. He didn't know whether to be in awe of what he had heard or suspicious. He would wait till after their second call before saying anything to anyone.

After Dorothy had spoken to Serafin, she sat on the couch and stared in disbelief at what she was seeing of the victim's demise. A surge of emotions overwhelmed her, primarily anger and sadness. What more barbaric murder could there be than the brutal rape of a little girl? Slowly she diverted her energies as much as possible away from the horror and toward finding the murderer. She felt she could find the animal that committed the rape, and she determined she would.

Dorothy was somewhat suspicious of Serafin, though. She had sensed his abruptness and nervousness and wondered if he was really heading the investigation. She called Lupo and asked him to check out Serafin that afternoon.

Later that evening Lupo verified that Serafin was detective lieutenant of the force.

"If it's a major case," Lupo conjectured, "he probably is involved."

Dorothy knew it was a major case. She decided to call Serafin the next morning and apologize for being suspicious.

"Suspicious of me?" Serafin laughed uncomfortably. What a bitch, he thought to himself.

"Don't be so surprised," Dorothy challenged him. "I didn't trust you, and you obviously were feeling the same thing about me."

They talked for a few minutes about the case. Dorothy told him that she still saw the murderer as a man in his late teens or early twenties. She reiterated that he drank a lot and added that he smoked dope. She also saw a pair of crutches or a wheelchair somewhere.

"Someone close to either the victim or the murderer is either on crutches or in a wheelchair. You have to know that I often confuse facts regarding the murderer and the victim. So, you have to think of both."

Dorothy took the birth date of the Pisces victim and said she wanted to think about the case a little more and that Serafin should call again at the end of the week.

It was during their third conversation that Dorothy said the little girl's first name began with a "K"—"something like Katherine," she said.

"What about the last name?" The now more relaxed, but obstinately skeptical Serafin pursued.

"Her last name? Well, I get something that reminds me of a beer."

"A beer? I don't get it," he said.

"A beer. Yes, I know. Like that upstate beer. Gennessee beer. Her last name has double letters in it, like Gennessee."

Serafin was again amazed. He was glad that he had everything on tape, as no one would believe him otherwise.

By their next telephone communication Serafin was feeling comfortable with the energetic psychic. He found her sympathetic and hardworking. He was impressed with her knowledge of police work and investigative procedure. She sympathized with his having to take second straw on the case to the FBI. She knew how the bureaucracies worked and which agency had power over the other.

At the end of their fifth talk Serafin suggested that he and the prosecutor visit Dorothy at her home and work on the case. Dorothy agreed and the following Thursday was settled upon.

"Could I bring you anything?" Serafin asked.

"Yes, something that belonged to the girl. I would like to hold onto something that she either wore or liked a lot."

Serafin agreed and said good-bye. He knew that he would have to tell the chief what he was doing, as someone would have to pay the psychic's fees. He explained to his superior what had occurred during the phone conversations he had had with the Nutley woman and that he had taped the conversations corroborating everything he had said.

The chief was surprised and amused. Having no sense of how much a psychic would charge for investigative work, he okayed the payment of anything up to $500.

Next Serafin went to the young parents of Kathy Hennessy and told them about his dealing with Dorothy. They had no objection, although they had no idea what could be accomplished by using a psychic. They consented to parting with some of Kathy's possessions, as long as they would be returned.

John Hennessy and his sister-in-law had cleaned out Kathy's drawers after the funeral. The only thing they had noticed missing was a favorite necklace Kathy always wore. Her father speculated it must have fallen off the day of the murder, or been ripped from her body.

Carol Hennessy placed into a brown paper bag Kathy's little plastic typewriter, one of her favorite toys, with her unfinished story still in the carriage; a doll's dress from Kathy's favorite doll; plus, a book and a Brownie pin.

Serafin asked his friend Neil Forte, the prosecutor in the Burlington County Prosecutor's Office, to accompany him on his adventure to Nutley. Forte, a young dark-haired, athletically built man, thought the invitation too intriguing to refuse.

"We'll go up in my Chevy," Serafin said. "I just had it tuned up last week."

The two men spent most of the two hours driving to Nutley anticipating what Dorothy would be like. Both men projected images of a mysterious woman, with the usual trappings of a bizarre mystic. But Serafin's discussions with Dorothy had already proved to him that she had abilities that could only be classified as extraordinary. He was not yet willing to let go of his skepticism, however.

Jason barked madly from the front window as a greeting to the nervous pair from southern New Jersey. Dorothy quickly led the animal into the basement and ran to the door to let in Serafin and Forte. Dressed in black slacks and a loose orange blouse, Dorothy did not suggest the looks or the spirit of a witch. The trio went into the kitchen, where Serafin set up his tape recorder and nervously watched the Italian seer as she opened packages of sweet rolls and made coffee for the men.

The first thing the Pemberton detective brought up was the fact that he had only $500 to spend, and he could go no higher. They were amazed to hear that Dorothy would accept no payment for her work, "especially with a child like this."

Dorothy sat down. First she took the Brownie pin Serafin handed her from the bag and held onto it for a moment while asking the men about the progress on the case. She was told they were watching several people, but that no suspects had yet been nabbed.

"Who is Margaret?" Dorothy asked.

"I don't know," Serafin said.

"She has something to do with the little girl. I feel that Margaret was in trouble. Maybe in trouble with Kathy? Does that register anything?" she asked.

Serafin responded negatively.

"What about Kathy's brother? Have you interrogated him?" Dorothy asked.

151

"How did you know she had a brother?" the dark-haired prosecutor asked.

"I see a little boy with the girl. That's how I know," Dorothy answered.

Serafin handed Dorothy the dress, which he thought to be one actually worn by Kathy. Dorothy laughed.

"This is a doll's dress, you Polish nitwit," Dorothy kidded the man. "She'd have to be pretty tiny to fit into this."

Serafin pulled out the typewriter from the bottom of the bag. While Dorothy handled the dress and thought about her own favorite doll as a child, Serafin removed the paper from the typewriter and set the toy on the table. He read the contents of Kathy's story.

As he read, he got noticeably excited. "I think I've just found Margaret and your trouble," he announced. "This is what Kathy had typed the day of her murder. It's a story about a girl named Margaret and how she had been sent home for being bad."

Now both men began to take note with avid tenacity of everything Dorothy said. Margaret, it turned out, lived four doors away from Kathy.

"I get another Margaret, as well," Dorothy continued. "Someone named Margaret Fox . . ."

"What about Margaret Fox?" Neil Forte interrupted her.

"I don't know. I've got to find something out about Margaret Fox. I don't know why, but I see Margaret Fox."

It was obvious that Forte knew Margaret Fox, but he came forth with nothing more than a question.

"Do you get a middle name on her?" he asked.

Dorothy thought for a moment. "It has double letters in it. Like Ellen."

Forte blanched. "Margaret Ellen Fox is the right name," he told them.

Margaret Ellen Fox had been kidnapped five years before. The case had never been resolved. The Burlington, New Jersey, teen-ager had been baby-sitting one evening, and was never seen again. Elements of the case had never been publicly disclosed; it was a case that had stayed on Forte's mind for these five years.

"It's not really pertinent to this case," Forte finally said.

"Let's go on, and maybe some other time we can work on that one."

Dorothy looked through fifteen mug shots and composites that Serafin handed her. None of the posed, lifeless stares triggered anything.

"I now get an older man as the murderer. I don't know why, but I get a man who is forty or fifty." She paused for a moment. "He wears glasses and I think a wig."

Serafin was confused, but he said nothing.

"If I wanted to get to this man's house from where Kathy was killed, I would head for where the balloons are."

"Balloons?" both men asked.

"I don't mean little balloons. I can't get the word right. Like the Hindenberg," she offered.

"Dirigibles?" Neil Forte asked. Serafin immediately thought of the Lakehurst Naval Air Station where blimps were assembled. That was less than thirty miles north of Pemberton Township.

"This man has been in the navy," Dorothy continued. "Highly decorated, too. He's been involved in cases like this before, doing things with kids like this one."

She went on to say that she saw a brown house, one that was entered not in the front, but through the side, and was to be found on a dead-end street. The house, she added, had a statue in the backyard. "Not Saint Anthony," she said, smiling.

The man, she said, had spent much time in California.

"Is this the man who murdered Kathy Hennessy?" Serafin tried to pin her down.

"I'm not sure. For some reason I'm getting this guy strongly. I've got to go on my feelings."

"Could his name be Harry?" Serafin asked, trying to locate a suspect he knew that might fit Dorothy's description.

"Not his first name. Maybe it's his middle name," Dorothy responded.

Awhile later Dorothy looked at Neil Forte and asked him if he were uncomfortable. The man said he was fine. Dorothy told him she felt he was having trouble with his feet, that they were bothering him. He blushed slightly and assured her that he was fine.

153

"Well, if they're not fine, they'll be better in a few days," she said and dropped the subject.

It was nearing three in the morning when Serafin and Forte kissed Dorothy and left her quiet neighborhood. As they departed, Dorothy told them they would be getting a major break in the case that day, perhaps within the next several hours.

The exhausted detectives were fascinated by all that had happened at Dorothy's. In the privacy of the car Forte told Serafin that he had been embarrassed by her questions about his feet. He had been to a foot doctor the previous day, he admitted, for a rash that he had picked up in Vietnam and could not cure.

"It's been fine for six months," he said, "and suddenly last weekend it reappeared."

Serafin decided to take the parkway south to Bricktown, which was slightly out of their way, but less confusing for him. Earlier they had gotten lost driving to Nutley. As Serafin drove, topping seventy-five miles an hour on the parkway, he saw the lights of a car parked at a dark gas station along the road. He knew the car belonged to a cop, and since he didn't want the hassle of explaining his way out of a ticket, he slowed down. As they drove past the station, his generator and oil lights suddenly flared. Serafin was shocked because the car had just been tuned up.

At the same time the police car pulled out of the gas station, drove behind Serafin, and then, with a sudden burst, passed him. Serafin flashed him down, blinking his lights off and on. Both cars stopped; Serafin got out and introduced himself to the black patrolman.

The men looked under the hood of the Chevy and discovered a broken fan belt. The patrolman said he would call the local police and have a tow truck sent out. Serafin suggested they bring a fan belt with them and gave the cop the correct size.

While they waited for the tow to arrive, and Neil Forte lay sleeping in the rear of Serafin's car, the helpful cop asked if Serafin was involved in the case concerning the raped girl. Serafin told him that he was in charge of the investigation for the Pemberton police and that they had

154

been working that evening on the case. He said nothing about Dorothy.

The cop had read about the case and had wondered if any men in Lakehurst had been interrogated, as it was certainly within the radius of suspicion. Serafin said he didn't think so. Then the tall, slow-moving patrolman said he had a man in mind, that even though he himself was not a detective, he felt this man should be considered.

Serafin thought for a moment. "His name wouldn't be Harry, would it?" he asked.

"Not his first name. It is his middle name, though," the policeman replied.

With that, Serafin ran to his car and woke up his slumbering colleague, telling him about the conversation he was having.

The two men returned to the waiting cop, as the tow appeared out of the darkness. As they repaired the fan belt, they talked about the case.

"I've known this guy for years," the cop said. "Ever since he moved here from California. In fact, we just indicted him for fooling around with kids."

"A big case?" Forte asked.

"No. Small shit. Started out with parents coming in and complaining. This guy hangs around the tennis courts a lot, bothers the kids."

"Describe this man," Serafin said.

"Oh, he's weird. He's one of those clean nuts, E-maculate," he said, adding extra emphasis to the beginning of the word. "Always well dressed. Wears one of them hair pieces . . ."

"How old is this man?" Serafin pressed.

"I think in his late forties. He works at one of the bases. Retired. He's got one of those cushy jobs saved for guys who retire with a lot of medals."

Serafin and Forte stood in the early morning light, goosebumps crawling over their bodies.

"What color house does this guy live in?" Serafin went on. The cop was beginning to think Serafin's questions were slightly crazy, but he continued, anyway.

"If I'm not wrong, his house is brown," the cop said, starting to edge away toward his own car.

"How do you get into his house?" Serafin followed him.

"What do you mean, how do you get into his house? Aren't these questions kind of funny for someone you know nothing about?" he finally retorted.

"I know it sounds weird, but if you'd just answer, I'll explain some other time. How do you get into the house?" he asked again.

The man stood and thought alongside the road. "Well," he finally said, "you go through this side porch. The front part is blocked off."

"Holy Christ," Serafin exclaimed.

Both Serafin and Forte shook the man's hand, asking him to leave word with a detective to call Serafin at his office in Pemberton the next morning. Both cars drove into the misty light, as the new day began to brighten the skies.

When Pat Serafin awakened to the cries of her one-year-old daughter early that morning, she was surprised to find her husband awake and sitting on the den couch, smoking a cigarette. He had not slept, he told her, because his mind was full of wonder at the evening's happenings. Pat was looking forward to meeting the Nutley phenomenon. "Soon," her weary husband told her, "she'll come here."

The lieutenant detective who phoned at Serafin's request was equally intrigued by the story Serafin unfolded that morning. Asking the detective to listen and see if he could discern anyone he knew, Serafin described the man in question according to Dorothy's vision.

"How do you know this guy?" the detective asked Serafin.

"Everything is from the psychic. She even mentioned that the guy has some sort of statue in his backyard. Does that fit any of your descriptions?"

The man was silent for a moment, taking in a long, thoughtful haul of his cigarette. "Serafin, this is amazing. The guy my cop was telling you about has some kind of Buddha in his backyard. How in hell did she know that?" he wondered.

Serafin went on to say that Dorothy said the man in question had been arrested before. The other detective confirmed that their suspect had been arrested, but not on anything big.

"How come I've never read anything about this man?" Serafin inquired.

"There's a reason for that," Snoopy declared. "This guy has some real good connections."

Serafin was convinced that Dorothy could not have read about the man whose middle name was "Harry" in the newspapers.

It was that afternoon that a weary Serafin drove to the FBI office at Fort Dix to inform FitzWilliam, the agent in charge of the investigation, of all that had transpired with Dorothy. Serafin was not expecting the reaction he received.

FitzWilliam, a middle-aged, handsome, graying man in a business suit, greeted the police officer warmly. The two men had spent enough moments at loggerheads on investigative issues to know where the other man stood. FitzWilliam listened with interest to all that Serafin reported, especially that the woman had worked on the Hearst case under the aegis of the FBI. He intended to check that out with Washington.

He made clear to Serafin that the Bureau's official stance on using psychics was negative. As far as he was concerned, they weren't viable investigative sources. However, in light of present facts, he would personally see to it that any expenses incurred would be handled by him, under other names, of course. He could hardly request funds for "psychic use."

Serafin thanked him and told him about Dorothy's attitude toward payment. "All she wants is a badge and a letter of commendation if the things she sees turn out to be true," Serafin proudly said in her defense.

Before Serafin left FitzWilliam, the stern-looking agent said that he would put the man Serafin was suspicious of under surveillance. Serafin was amazed and thankful for the man's support.

Dorothy agreed to visit Pemberton Township on the following Saturday morning. FitzWilliam said he would like to follow Serafin around.

"We'll stay behind you in another car," he said cautiously. "There's no reason for us to work directly with her."

Serafin was miffed by the man's attitude, but he knew he had no choice. He knew that he, too, would be watched by his superiors. His belief in Dorothy was still tenuous when challenged, and that didn't please him.

Pemberton Township is sixty-five square miles of mostly rural land, full of nineteenth-century wooden houses interspersed with neighborhoods of geometric military architecture. When Dorothy and Bob Allison drove through the community on that Saturday morning in March, they felt it had more greenery and more charm than the area's crime rate had led them to imagine.

Serafin met them at an appointed spot and left their car at the police station, asking Dorothy whether she could direct them to the Hennessys' home, where the FBI was awaiting them. Unfortunately the Hennessys themselves were not around, having been called to Delaware where Carol's sister lived.

Dorothy told the police that she would like to direct them to the house, but that they should not expect a direct hit; a margin of a block should be allowed. Within thirty minutes Dorothy pointed to a small, red brick house with a carport, announcing that it was Kathy's home. She was correct.

When they got underway, Serafin was quieter and more skeptical than Dorothy had expected. The reason, she knew, was the car that was following them without introduction, waiting in judgment. She was being tested.

First Dorothy said she would lead them to where Kathy's body had been found. Not wanting to waste time, she described to Serafin the route she would take.

"From the street we're on, you go to a street that looks like a dead end, but it's not," she said. "Go off the end of that street and you'll be on a dirt road that should lead to water. The lake, I guess."

Serafin understood her perfectly.

"When you get to the dirt road, you go to the right. There should be a dirt path with a log across it. I saw that

158

log when I saw Kathy the first time. Her body was right near there," she concluded.

Dorothy's intuition was easing Serafin's insecurity. As he worked with her, he began to resent the FBI's attitude.

After they had all driven around the area in which the girl's body was found, Dorothy said she wanted to describe an event that had occurred some years before. She wanted to go to a spot where a little boy had drowned and a pair of eyeglasses had been found. The water had been too shallow for drowning, she said, but the case had never been solved.

Serafin thought he knew which case she was seeing, and trusting her sight, he took her to the spot. The large green Ford LTD followed close behind.

Next Dorothy described a road that would fork. By taking the turn to the right, one would pass two pillars. Serafin knew this to be the entrance to Fort Dix, which bordered on the area in which the body was discovered.

Dorothy didn't know whether she was looking for the murderer, or sensing something about someone else who might be involved with the case. She then described a cemetery.

"There are two cemeteries in the area," Serafin told her.

"This one is very old, as old as the oldest houses here," Dorothy said. "I don't think it's still used. Anyway, this one would be near or next to a runway for airplanes."

The description could not have been more exact. Serafin knew it to be the old Pointville Cemetery that predated the military installation, and that couldn't be moved when the runways were constructed at McGuire.

From the cemetery Dorothy got a strong sense of someone standing on a ladder to paint. The cops told her that painting was being done by dozens of men daily on the installation.

"No, that's not it," she warned. "We're going to run into a painter soon."

Next she told the detectives she wished to find a church in the area where drugs once had been found in the bushes. The incident, if it had occurred, meant nothing to Serafin or any of his men. He decided to chance it and ask the FBI if they knew of anything similar that might have occurred on the base.

Serafin had to explain to FitzWilliam, who wondered at all the circuitous ambling that had been done, what reasons had been behind all the previous stops. Leading up to the church story, he said that he was presently stumped and had come to them for help. He told them what Dorothy had described.

"How in the hell did she know about that?" one of the agents said.

Serafin smiled, pleased at the reaction. "She's been doing this all day. You might enjoy talking to her sometime."

FitzWilliam ignored the policeman's gibe and requested that Dorothy be asked, first, if she saw who had been involved with the drugs.

Moments later Serafin bounced back to the official green car and announced that Dorothy felt someone working for the church had been responsible.

"She's right on that one. It was the assistant chaplain," FitzWilliam conceded. "We locked him up for possession of heroin that was found in a bag in the bushes."

From the church, which they drove to, Dorothy asked to be taken to the tower on the airstrip. As they walked on the asphalt surface around the air tower, Dorothy pointed to a large building not far away.

"The guy I'm describing works in that building," Dorothy said.

Once again Dorothy had correctly led the investigation to the man whose middle name was "Harry" and whose life and home she had so accurately depicted. Serafin went back to the FBI annex-on-wheels and informed the men that Dorothy had correctly pointed them to the building in which their suspect worked. He did not, however, inform Dorothy that she was correct.

Driving back toward Browns Mills, the sergeant riding in the back seat pointed to an empty lot and asked Dorothy if she knew what had once been there. Slightly agitated by the games she was being put through, she directed herself into the past and smiled.

"You son of a bitch," she said, poking the man in the stomach, "that was your old police station." Nine years

scribed fit the bill of David Geary. The other person Serafin suspected was an old school friend of Carol Hennessy named Phil, who lived in Pennsylvania and whom John had gotten to know well.

Phil had been expected on that fatal Saturday, but had never appeared or called to say he wasn't coming. An intelligent, handsome young man, Phil had a reputation for being volatile. Little Spanky had even mentioned that Phil had beaten Kathy for being bad, although no one else had ever seen him beat the children. Serafin knew that a "beating," in the eyes of a child, could cover anything from a slap on the rear to a punching.

It was impossible, Carol Hennessy insisted, that one of her oldest friends would hit her children in a drastic manner, much less be capable of the murder. She would hear nothing of the matter.

But the police could not discount the possibilities. In any investigation the family or friends of those involved are open to suspicion. These could include people so completely trusted that they were often underfoot in the victim's home. In fact, many a criminal investigation has been contaminated by allowing too much traffic in such a home.

At the end of Dorothy's day in Pemberton, the investigation had seemingly moved nowhere. The man she had psychically pursued probably had nothing to do with the Hennessy case, but all admitted that she had found a man the police believed to be a child molester from her home a hundred miles north.

The chief of police in the suspect's area refused to have the man in the brown house confronted merely on the suspicions of a psychic. The man was eventually interviewed, however, by Serafin and Forte. His alibi for March 6 was solid and beyond suspicion. They would no longer look at him as a suspect.

After a barbeque at the Serafins' home, Dorothy and her husband drove north to Nutley, exhausted from the tensions and apprehensions of the day. Dorothy would make one more trip to the town, since she wanted to meet Kathy's parents, to see if she could derive any other feelings from them. Most particularly Dorothy was anxious to meet

Spanky, whom everyone insisted knew nothing, but whom Dorothy had seen in one of her visions as "the boy in the bushes."

Dorothy felt depressed working on the Hennessy case. Her personal philosophy, however, was to keep her worries and sadness hidden. She had learned from being in numerous traumatized environments that her own personal emotions were best left for herself to handle, for better or worse. She would never let Serafin or the Hennessys see anything but the compassion she had for the family and the murdered victim, who had become part of the fabric of her soul.

Serafin felt sad, too, working on the case. Each time he would look at his own little girl, a silent prayer would cross his lips. He had grown fond of Dorothy, welcoming her humor and candor. In her brief stay she had managed to amaze a bevy of skeptics.

While Dorothy was working on the Hennessy case, one of the many calls she received for help was from a Greek family in Baltimore. On March 15, thirteen-year-old Gus Karavasalis disappeared. His parents, who had moved to the United States three years earlier, were frantic in a strange land and without sufficient resources.

The state police, who had handled the case originally, had turned it over to the Youth Division of the Baltimore County Police, where Detective Al Darden, a lively, warm twenty-five-year-old patrolman now had charge of the case with fellow detective Bill Bendetto.

Dorothy had worked with the Baltimore County Police Department the year before in trying to discover the identity of a girl's corpse that had been found along a road. When she received their call asking for help on the Karavasalis case, she was glad to oblige, having been treated kindly and with respect by the department. Also, as soon as she heard Darden discuss the missing teen-ager, she began to get strong positive feelings.

"Wait, don't tell me too much," she stopped him. "I'm already getting vibes. That kid is alive and well. Don't give up," she said. "I'll have to come to Baltimore. I'm working on a case down in Pemberton Township next weekend, and I'll come to Baltimore after that. Tell the parents the kid is alive," she commanded Darden.

The Youth Division had a lot of work on its hands, with 1,944 runaways in Maryland that year alone. After ten days of looking for Gus, absolutely no information seemed to lead anywhere. But Darden took hope in Dorothy's promise that Gus was still alive.

Dark, hirsute, and mature looking, Gus could easily pass for a teen-ager of eighteen or nineteen. The shy, diffident boy had run into some problems in school, having been caught smoking cigarettes earlier that fall. His family was brought before the assistant principal where Gus's aunt acted as interpreter for the non-English-speaking parents.

Gus Karavasalis's parents were given to understand that their son would be sent to reform school if he were caught smoking again. Gus was humiliated that he had embarrassed his parents and caused them discomfort. Then, in March, he disappeared after getting caught again with a cigarette on school grounds.

The despairing parents, who sat every night before their window silently hoping a miracle would return their son, had to rely on the help of the police and their detectives. They had seen the Nutley psychic on a television interview and begged the police to call her. The Youth Division was responsive to their needs, Darden and Bendetto working closely with the family. Alex, Gus's eighteen-year-old brother, searched almost daily with the police.

The Greek community of Baltimore rallied to help the family. Everything was tried: newspapers, fliers, television, police, even the Cherry Pickers of Essex tried to help, but to no avail. Thousands of leads were received, but nothing came of them.

Dorothy was excited to work on a case in which she felt certain the missing person was alive. It was seldom that a case came her way involving a missing person who had left of his own volition, or a kidnap victim who was still alive. In the next six months she would travel to Baltimore more than a dozen times. Bob, her husband, also of Greek background, helped to assuage the fears of the Karavasalis family. Dorothy's assurance that their son was still alive infused them with enough strength to continue the search day after day, month after month.

Before Dorothy returned to Pemberton Township, she spent some time trying to discern more about the man she felt was the murderer. She reported to Serafin on the phone that she felt the young man lived in a trailer park, that he had been in jail before, that he was adopted or had a foster mother. Moreover he had never graduated from high school, had a hot temper, and someone near to him was either on crutches or in a wheelchair.

Dorothy's descriptions at the moment seemed to lead directly to David Geary. When questioned by the FBI, Geary had played it cool and aloof, stating that he had been visiting his family the day of the murder. But Geary did live in a trailer, with a couple who drank heavily and refused to answer questions.

Two things especially piqued Serafin's interest regarding Geary: first, the fact that the woman who lived in the trailer with him was in a wheelchair, and second, that Geary had visited John Hennessy on several occasions, selling him medicinal herbs like Tai Sticks.

Serafin told the young parents that Dorothy felt Spanky knew something. John Hennessy had tried several times to place his son's location at the time of the murder. Everyone knew the two children were practically inseparable. Why had Spanky left his sister on that day?

John Hennessy did feel that Spanky must have been to the crime scene because he knew exactly where to lead his father when the pair had walked in the woods the day after Kathy's murder.

Dorothy suggested that the boy be brought to Dr. Ribner's office for hypnosis. John and Carol were willing, wanting to uncover any horrors that might be blocked by their son's emotions. But the FBI wouldn't allow it. They felt Ribner might be in cahoots with the psychic. If hypnosis was the next game plan, they would supply the doctor.

Spanky was taken to a New York child psychologist who specialized in hypnotic therapy. The session, which lasted thirty minutes and cost the FBI $500, proved fruitless. The specialist announced that the boy was not susceptible to hypnosis. In a teletype to headquarters the agents reported to their superiors that policeman Serafin was responsible for the hypnosis idea, and that any further sessions would be on his shoulders.

It was the following Saturday that Dorothy and her son, Paul, drove to Pemberton Township. Paul was in high school and had come to enjoy his mother's investigative jaunts. They drove directly to the Hennessys' home, where Carol and John awaited them with Serafin.

Dorothy arrived with gifts for the little boy. She hugged the parents as if they had been longtime friends, careful not to be morose in Spanky's company.

As they sat around the sunny den, Dorothy felt Spanky was on the verge of telling them something. He had been climbing on Paul's lap and then looking around at the adults, as if something was on his mind. Dorothy mentioned this to Serafin in confidence.

Moments later the little boy, dressed in a T-shirt and shorts, climbed into Dorothy's lap. She smiled and gently bumped him up and down, laughing and talking with him. Suddenly Spanky stopped playing and threw his arms around Dorothy's neck.

"I had a bad dream," he whispered in her ear. Dorothy felt her heart stop, anticipating what the little boy was about to say.

She sat him up straight in her lap and gently coaxed him into telling her the dream.

"What was the dream about?" she softly asked.

"It was about my friend," he told her.

"Oh. And who is your friend?" Dorothy asked.

"My girl friend. Her name is Margaret," Spanky said. John and Carol, along with Serafin and Paul, stood breathlessly watching Dorothy gently assuage the fears and horrors that the little boy held within him. Tears began to form in his mother's eyes. Dorothy knew she would have to remain strong.

Spanky told her that he had been playing in the woods with his friend. Playing with sticks and throwing rocks at a tree. But his friend left him to go off and play with some-one else.

"Who was the other person?" Dorothy asked.

"A man. A mean man. He hit my friend." Spanky was suddenly on his feet, jumping up and down.

"He hit her and jumped on her," the child screamed.

Dorothy grabbed Spanky in her arms. "What did you do, Spanky? Don't worry, everything is okay."

"I ran to my Daddy, but he was sleeping," Spanky said.

"Why didn't you wake him up?" Dorothy pursued.

"I couldn't," he said.

"What did you do then?"

"I ran back . . ."

"Back where?"

"To the bushes. I went to the bushes. I didn't want any-one to hurt me," he told Dorothy, trembling with fear.

Spanky sat wrapped in Dorothy's embrace, describing what he saw. He said that Margaret had mud on her knees. One moment she was on all fours, playing like a pig. Her eyes were closed, he said, and the man jumped on her be-hind.

Carol Hennessy left the room. Tears streamed down Ser-afin's face as he leaned against the front door, averting his glance.

Again Spanky jumped from Dorothy's reach and shouted as if he had a gun in his hand. "Bam bam," he shot. "Bambambambam," his imaginary gun shot into the air.

"I shot the man! I shot him! I shot him!" the boy re-peated, until Dorothy grabbed him and again he climbed in her lap. John Hennessy, his eyes unblinking, was in shock. Serafin had gone into the kitchen and was phoning the FBI, briefly telling them what had just transpired in the Hennessy den.

Was Spanky talking from a dream? Had he seen the rape and murder of his own sister? When his father asked him to describe the man Margaret was with, Spanky said he couldn't remember. Later he began to change details of the story, embellishing it with fantastic details.

It was decided, after FitzWilliam had arrived and they had walked Spanky into the sylvan area where he led them directly over the log and to the spot where his sister was found, that another stab at hypnosis might be in order.

Serafin, Dorothy, her son, John Hennessy, and Spanky drove to Manhattan to Ribner's Central Park office. The doctor greeted the entourage with a sucker for Spanky. He led Spanky into his inner sanctum and sat the boy down. With his father and Dorothy talking gently to Spanky, Ribner was able to begin hypnotic suggestion. Spanky, as is often the case with children, could only reach a certain level of the process, a relaxed level between waking and sleeping.

Ribner and Dorothy led the boy down the trail of his dream. At first much of the story was the same as he had reported to Dorothy. But after awhile he seemed to conjure happenings that were more and more improbable, mixing realities he had overheard from adult conversations with childlike perceptions. The doctor, however, was convinced the boy had witnessed the crime in the woods. No murderer would be locked up from Spanky's recollection or dream, however.

Dorothy, too, was then hypnotized. John and Spanky went downstairs to sit in Central Park while Serafin and Ribner tried to determine if Dorothy could get closer to the criminal. She could not. She did, however, begin to describe another suspect.

She said he was young and worked alone a great deal. "He has lots of little glass bottles in his basement. It's like a dark workshop." She went on to say that she sensed he had problems with girls: they made him nervous. "In order to get to Kathy's," she told the two men, "he would have to drive a long distance. He doesn't live in New Jersey."

Serafin felt strongly that the description Dorothy gave was of the Hennessy's friend, Phil. He would have to broach the subject with John Hennessy, who had not known Phil as long as his wife had.

After the session the group proceeded north to Nutley, and Dorothy's home. She left Serafin and John to be entertained by Bob, and Justine took Spanky in hand, leading him upstairs to play while Dorothy prepared dinner. Serafin, in the meantime, began to ask John specific questions about Phil.

"Does he have hobbies?" Serafin inquired.

"He has spent a helluva lot of money on chemistry equipment," John said. "Lots of stuff in his basement that he never touches. He's that type. Starts something and doesn't finish."

While Serafin became more and more suspicious of Phil, little Spanky was unraveling another fantasy upstairs.

Justine and Spanky were playing on the CB radio. The boy enjoyed playing with the radio buttons and flashing lights, and he especially liked holding the microphone. As soon as he got hold of it, he began talking about his "friend being hurt" again. Justine, realizing what was spewing forth, clicked on the cassette recorder.

Justine encouraged the boy to tell her the story as he spoke into the CB radio, pretending to be a policeman at one moment, then a radio announcer, interjecting the story with "beeping" sounds.

"Spanky, tell me who the man is," Justine coaxed.

"He's a bad guy. He's Phil. I don't like him," Spanky said with a scowl.

Justine, slightly jolted by the actual naming of a man, told Spanky to continue playing with the radio while she went to see if her mother needed any help in the kitchen. Justine went downstairs and asked Serafin, in a quiet voice, if she might have a word with him privately. She created as little stir as possible, not wanting to ignite a situation with Spanky's father.

Justine told Serafin what had occurred upstairs with Spanky. The detective was astonished at the accusation against Phil. He knew, however, that Spanky's mind might have been picking up undercurrents in the adult conversations, as Phil had been mentioned several times during the day. But the incident did add fuel to his growing suspicion.

After Dorothy's dinner Serafin told John on the drive back to Pemberton that he wanted to have a talk with Phil. John agreed, trying not to question the detective's request, as he knew his wife would.

John Hennessy had grown up with enough experiences to know that the complexities of the mind and personality were more than deceptive. The mere fact that most of the suspects in his daughter's murder were friends or acquaintances of his made him search far into his conscience and question his view of life. His own daughter killed by a "friend." He would be glad to leave New Jersey and the tragedies of the past thirty days.

John Hennessy made the arrangements with Phil to come to Pemberton while he and Carol and Spanky would be in Delaware for the day, so the investigation could be conducted without family interference. Carol was not fully appraised of Serafin's intention to interrogate her friend for the second time and this time with a sharper purpose.

Standing erect and confident, the young man shook hands with Serafin and Detective Mathers, a husky, dark-haired man with a prominent moustache. Before any discussion began, Serafin asked Phil to sit down and he explained that he had some questions he wanted to put to him, and that he should be fully aware of his rights, which the detective then related.

Phil, crossing one leg over another and fidgeting with his fingers, told the two men he had been reading books about pedophilia and crimes of sexual nature. He conjectured that the person they would be looking for had to have had a grudge against his father. He spoke about the psychology of such criminals, pointing out that most of them keep something that belongs to the victim, like a bracelet or a necklace.

Serafin remembered Dorothy's mentioning a piece of jewelry near where Kathy was found. She had seen it earlier, during one of their first conversations. He wondered if any of Kathy's jewelry was missing.

Serafin asked Phil where he had been the day of the murder.

"Everyone thought you were heading here," he said. "Where did you go?"

"I stayed home," Phil replied. "I couldn't get it together to drive here and back the same day."

"Why didn't you let anyone know?" Mather inquired, leaning forward in his seat.

"I don't have to let anyone know," Phil snapped. "These people are my friends. I don't have to explain myself all the time."

"Right now we'd like you to explain yourself," Serafin said.

"I'll bet Carol doesn't even know you're talking to me. That's why she's not here, right?" Phil stared at the two men. "If you think I'd do something to her child, you're out of your mind. I can't believe this crap."

"We may be out of our minds, but it's our job to check into every possibility. I don't think Carol imagines for a second that you're capable of harming her children, at least not like I do. I think you could do it," Serafin challenged him.

"Murder a kid? You bastards are too much. She may have been too big for her britches sometimes, but I'm a sane man. I know the difference between an adult and a child. Sure, she might have thought she was an adult sometimes, and she needed a smack once in a while . . ."

"How many times have you smacked her?" Mathers asked.

"Smacked her? Who said I ever hit her?" Phil searched for solid ground.

"Spanky said you hit them," Serafin said calmly.

"That little bastard doesn't know what he's talking about. How can you listen to a little kid?" Phil asked. "Would you put someone away on a child's testimony? Never. Especially not one who lies all the time." Phil was desperate.

"If you're so innocent, then go on the box. Let's have an objective look at your reasoning and alibi. That's all I ask," Serafin said.

Phil thought for a moment, angered and frightened by the accusations. Finally he agreed to the polygraph test, thinking that the Hennessys would make such a fuss when they found out, the test would never be administered.

When Carol and John heard of the details of the meeting between Phil and Serafin, they were incensed. For days Serafin stayed clear of the Hennessy house, waiting for Carol to cool down before trying to explain his position. In the meantime it was John Hennessy who had to defend his decision to allow the meeting to take place.

Serafin did meet with Carol and John on the following Wednesday evening. He told the angry woman that he wasn't happy having to pursue channels of thought that placed her friend in an unfavorable light, but he had no choice but to pursue him. He told the parents what Dorothy had seen in her session at Ribner's, describing Phil. But it was when he told the parents that their own son had said that Phil was the "bad man" he had seen with "his friend" that Carol Hennessy broke down in tears.

The mother was more distraught than she had been at any time since Kathy's burial. That one of her oldest friends was being accused of her child's murder left her speechless. She knew that Phil had psychological problems, but the most she would say to Serafin was that he might need help.

Serafin then asked if Kathy usually wore any jewelry.

"Yes. A gold chain," Carol told him. "She always wore the gold chain my parents gave her."

"Did you find the necklace?" Serafin asked.

"No, not that I recall." It was John who spoke. "It wasn't on Kathy's body, and when we cleaned out her things, we couldn't find it anywhere. We even checked in Spanky's drawers to see if it had been misplaced, and we found nothing."

Serafin mentioned that Dorothy had seen a piece of jewelry in her vision of the murder. If the psychic was right, and Serafin's suspicions were accountable, Phil's would be the place to search for the missing necklace.

Since the meeting with Dorothy and the FBI in the courtroom, the psychic had held to her own belief that the man named David was the murderer. FitzWilliam agreed with her suspicion. Only Serafin still held to the notion that the family friend might be culpable.

Phil, clearly agitated and hurt, took the polygraph as planned. But his emotional condition made the entire examination useless. From that point on, Serafin's investigation shifted away from Phil, and there was never any confirmation of Spanky's charge that Phil had beaten Kathy. Nor did Dorothy gather any "psychic evidence" that the accusation was true.

The day after the exam Spanky appeared holding the gold chain necklace that had belonged to his sister. Where he had found it and how long he had had it, the little boy could not answer. Each imploring question was answered with a frightened shrug. The parents could only hope that he had not found it near his sister's body, as Dorothy had seen.

At the Hilltop Trailer Park, not a mile from the Hennessy house, David Geary entered the small office of the trailer camp owner, John Waters. Waters, a heavyset, deep-voiced former air force sergeant, had been having problems with the people Geary was living with and had begun the process of eviction. Complaints from neighbors that Geary and his friends were rowdy and noisy till late in the night settled the man's intent to have them off this property. Moreover they owed Waters back rent from several months.

Waters, his shirt unbuttoned to the waist, revealing a round bulge of hair, asked the thin-bearded Geary what he wanted.

"You're going to be getting your money," Geary said. "I'm working now, so cut the eviction crap." Geary had taken a job two weeks before as a cleaning man in a nearby factory.

"Forget it," Waters huffed. "I'll just keep doing what I was doing. I want you all out of here."

"I'm gonna punch your fucking face in," Geary moved forward and stopped, just beyond the reach of Waters's heavily muscled arms.

"You're out of your mind, mister. Get out of my office and off my property. You got no place here," Waters said.

Geary grabbed his collar. "You son of a bitch, you can't evict us. You got no grounds to complain."

Waters shoved Geary forward, pinning him against the desk, Geary's back arched like a taut bow.

"I'm going to cause you a great deal of trouble, Mr. David Geary. You shouldn't have come in here this morning. You will regret it forever," and Waters, letting go of the man, left the office.

He went directly to the police department, where he was directed to Serafin's office.

"You know that Geary fellow somebody interviewed me about awhile ago?" Waters stood before Serafin's desk, obviously angry. "Don't you have him as a suspect in that little kid's murder?"

"Yeah, he's one of the suspects, all right," Serafin leaned back.

"Well, I want to register a complaint with you. That little bastard tried to attack me this morning," Waters told Serafin. "I think that guy would kill anyone, even a little kid. He told me he'd get me."

Serafin was excited by the news. Whether or not the man's complaint was totally valid was not important. If they could get Geary behind bars for a couple of days before some judge set a low bail and let him out, they could question him. Serafin told Waters to sit tight for a moment, that he would call the county prosecutor's office and explain the situation.

Geary was locked up the following day for "threat to kill and assault and battery." The bail was set at $5,000, just high enough to keep him incarcerated for a while.

FitzWilliam was glad to hear Geary was in jail. Twice before the suspect had failed the polygraph and had eluded two intense interrogations by his men. This time the FBI man didn't want to lose an opportunity. He called Neil Forte in the county prosecutor's office and asked him to interrogate Geary.

The following day Neil Forte and his partner, Ed Eastwood, spent two hours in the prosecutor's office trying to break Geary's defenses. The suspect fidgeted like a rat in a closed maze. He checked the closet to see if anyone was hiding there, he refused to allow note-taking, he refused to answer questions he didn't want to answer.

Forte decided after a long round of questioning to let the man return to his cell for a couple of hours to think over the interrogation. They would meet again that afternoon.

On the walk back to his cell, Eastwood asked Geary a direct question.

"Why did you kill the kid?" the detective asked, hoping against hope that an answer would come.

"I didn't mean to kill her," Geary whispered, looking at the floor, walking down the corridor as if discussing his health.

Eastwood stopped. "You didn't mean to kill her . . . ?"

"I got into her," Geary said. "I didn't want her to die."

David Geary was sentenced to two life terms on March 7, 1978, what would have been Kathy Hennessy's ninth birthday.

Dorothy was relieved to hear of Geary's sentence. The Pemberton Police Department awarded her with a badge and made her an official member of the department. Dorothy had been awarded badges from many departments across the country, and she showed visitors her trophies with extreme pride. Serafin had a case made of oak with velvet backing for her badges, which she proudly displayed in her home and on television. The recognition and respect of the police was payment enough for her.

With another success tucked under her arm, she focused on several other cases she had been working on in Staten Island, Washington State, Minneapolis, and Baltimore.

It was in July when Dorothy began to get a clearer picture of the surroundings of the missing teen-ager, Gus Karavasalis. She had long ago decided that Gus had been moving around. She came to Baltimore more to be with the parents, who grew to depend on her and her husband for emotional support, than to find their son whom she knew was nowhere in the Baltimore area.

Under hypnosis she saw twin peaks and a lot of water. She felt that Gus was somewhere in the West. There was a large bridge near him. As she could not discern distances, she could not place how far away the bridge or water were.

Dorothy told them that the name Paul would play an important role in the case. She reported that Gus was close to fire, was with other Greeks, and was living in an area with hills all around and many bridges. She also saw him in a uniform.

It was not until November 2 that the family received word that Gus might indeed be alive. One of his former teachers, Paul Radecke, who had moved to California, recognized the teen-ager in a San Francisco coffee shop. Having heard of his disappearance, he wrote to a Baltimore teacher who passed the information along to Gus's parents.

Alex Karavasalis flew with his mother to San Francisco in search of Gus. Detective Bendetto, who had stayed close to the case for eight months, accompanied them to the West Coast.

By that time the former teacher had seen Gus a second time and relayed the information to them that he was in Berkeley. Dorothy's clues—that he was near fire and with other Greeks—led them to the Greek restaurant where Gus worked.

Gus had run away fearing he had dishonored his family and would be sent back to Greece by his father. He had left Baltimore with $40 in his pocket and a bus ticket to Miami. He had found Miami difficult, so he pawned his watch and ring and hitchhiked across the country to San Francisco.

He was hired as a cook in the Greek restaurant by a man who believed Gus was nineteen. He earned enough money to pay his share of rent where the Greek landlord also believed the fourteen-year-old boy was considerably older.

His uniform was as Dorothy had described, and the fire was the hot stove over which Gus worked every day. Most importantly Gus was alive and well, and greatly relieved to be returning to his family.

A joyous celebration was held, which Dorothy and Bob attended as special guests of honor.

"This was the happiest Thanksgiving of our lives," Gus's mother beamed. "Two hundred fifty-five days his bed was empty. Now it's finally full."

Chapter 7

Memorial Day, 1976

Dorothy handed the phone to her husband, cupping the receiver. "Take down the information from this woman," Dorothy whispered. "We're going to her house right now. She lives on Staten Island, wherever in God's territory that is. I'm getting strong feelings from this woman."

Ellen Jacobson, usually a lively woman, was practically inaudible on the phone. Calling Dorothy Allison had not been her idea, nor did she have any idea what a psychic could do to find her missing fourteen-year-old daughter, Susan.

But Ellen's sister, June, had heard about the Nutley psychic from a friend and had pressed her to call; in addition, a reporter from the Staten Island *Advance* had called, giving Ellen Dorothy's phone number through a mother Dorothy had worked with the previous year. The message included the information that "Dorothy was at home" that Memorial Day afternoon.

Reported missing on May 15, Susan Jacobson would be the longest, most arduous case on which Dorothy had worked; a case in which not only her own stamina, but also the grim perseverance of the young parents, Bill and Ellen Jacobson, would be pushed to an inhuman threshold.

Ellen Jacobson and her younger sister, June, were born on Staten Island of Scottish parents; both women had fair complexions and short, light brown hair. Ellen, thirty-seven, worked hard as the mother of seven children, whose ages spanned from one year to sixteen. No one ever felt unwelcome in Bill and Ellen's house, no matter how busy or chaotic the movements of their large family might be, because the parents worked closely and lovingly to keep their home open to strangers and friends.

When Bob and Dorothy got to the three-story Jacobson house, located on a corner in Staten Island, Dorothy felt an immediate kinship for the tall, energetic but nervous woman who greeted them. Dorothy could see the tear-stained eyes behind the tinted wire-framed glasses. After two weeks of constant vigilance and searching for her daughter, desperation was ingrained in Ellen's smile.

Dorothy gave the woman a hug—a gesture of deeply felt sympathy, for Dorothy, in her own mind, already knew that Ellen Jacobson's daughter had been murdered.

"Where's the coffee?" Dorothy asked as soon as the upstairs door closed behind them and they stood in the bright, small kitchen and dining area. Ellen Jacobson anxiously poured coffee all around.

"I'm sorry my husband isn't here," she said. "The reporter from the newspaper said I should call you right away, so I didn't have time to wait for Bill. He's out with friends looking for Susan. He doesn't usually give up till just before the sun goes down. There must be twenty people out there looking today."

Dorothy sat at the table and pulled out a note pad and pen. She began writing.

"I see 'MAR.' What is it? Do you know?" Dorothy asked Ellen.

"Can't imagine. Is it part of someone's name?" Ellen wondered.

"No, I don't think it's part of anything. I just see three letters, 'MAR,' and nothing else."

Dorothy wrote down the number '2562' and showed it to Ellen.

179

"Mean anything?" Dorothy probed.

"It's Susan's birthday," Ellen said, sounding slightly incredulous.

Dorothy wrote down "405–408," and again presented it to Ellen. The mother stopped for a moment to think and finally said that if the numbers were related to the birthday, then 4:05 would have been the correct time of Susan's birth.

"Good," Dorothy said. "I'm getting a lot of strong feelings, which I will describe to you first, and then, see if you can place them," Dorothy instructed her. "When I'm done, I'll ask you things about the case and the investigation."

Ellen grimaced at the word "investigation," but before she could say anything, Dorothy went on with her vision.

"I have a very good picture of an area related to Susan," Dorothy told Ellen. "I see twin bridges in the distance, but one of the bridges isn't for cars. The area is like a swamp. There's an abandoned car near the place where I see 'MAR.' I also see two sets of dual church steeples and two huge smokestacks. The 'MAR' will help us pinpoint where to begin. That's what we've got to find first."

Ellen's mind reeled with the facts. She was too frightened to fully comprehend anything Dorothy was saying. She knew that there were plenty of bridges and church steeples around the island, but her husband would be better equipped to help the psychic. He had already taken three weeks off from his work at Citibank in Manhattan to search for his second oldest daughter.

"Where're the police?" Dorothy asked suddenly.

Ellen shuddered at the question. Gus Doyle, June's boyfriend, had run an investigation of his own. Doyle, a tall, boisterous Irishman, worked as an insurance investigator and was fully schooled in the language of investigative procedures.

In addition to family and friends, help in the search for Susan had been provided by members of a citizens-band radio club, cabdrivers, and bus drivers. But in two weeks there had still been little investigation done by the police, as far as Bill and Ellen were concerned.

When Ellen had phoned the Staten Island police at 9:00

180

P.M. on Saturday, May 15, the answering policeman had been unsympathetic to her plight.

"A fourteen-year-old girl who is only missing three hours after dinner isn't missing at all," the man said. "She's out screwing around with friends."

"We've talked to all her friends," Ellen persisted. "Nobody has seen her since early this afternoon. I know she hasn't run away."

"That's what they all say," the officer exclaimed. "Okay, lady, relax. I'll have someone by your place in an hour to take down the facts." He hung up abruptly.

Someone did come. An officer appeared more than an hour later, asked very few questions, none of which had to do with Susan's physical description, and left. The next day Ellen was told by a detective on the phone that if Susan had not shown up by Monday, the case would be turned over to the Missing Persons Bureau, whose offices were in Manhattan.

For the next week, the Jacobsons heard nothing from the Missing Persons Bureau, and only briefly from the local police. On the seventh day they were informed by phone that they had to obtain a PINS (Persons in Need of Supervision) warrant, which Bill Jacobson did, spending an entire day in court to obtain it. But the PINS warrant merely emphasized the fact that the officials felt Susan had run away.

On the twelfth day after Susan's disappearance, Patricia, the oldest of the seven children, was sitting on the shady corner in front of her house when suddenly, a man in a business suit grabbed her arm and announced that he had "found" her.

"Found who?" Patricia screamed as she wrenched her arm free.

"Susan Jacobson," the man announced.

"You're crazy, mister. We may look alike, but I'm not Susan," the angry teen-ager snarled.

The man who had approached Patricia was a detective from the Missing Persons Bureau. After mistaking Patricia for Susan, he proceeded upstairs to introduce himself to the parents. The man sat with Bill and Ellen around their dining table for fifteen minutes, during which time he told them "everything possible would be done" to find Susan, but that "nine times out of ten these cases are runaways." He also asked some questions. He had heard Susan had a boyfriend: was he around?

Dempsey Hawkins was always around, usually on the corner in front of the Jacobsons' house with the other neighborhood kids. Ellen told the investigator that he might find him there now.

The man requested a copy of Susan's dental chart, for possible future identification. Ellen gave him a flier of which Bill had made two thousand copies to be distributed all over Staten Island. That flier, with Susan's photograph on it, and the dental chart were the only things the parents saw go into their daughter's file.

The investigator did locate Dempsey on the street. A strapping, wiry-haired mulatto, Dempsey Hawkins glared at the fortyish man mistrustfully, as he glared at all the world. Born out of wedlock, Dempsey lived with his British mother and his sister in the Port Richmond neighborhood. Dempsey's life had been difficult, at best. He had grown up neither black nor white and had learned that taking the offense was a stronger position, ultimately, than defense. Confronting people, he presented a solid, sometimes stony facade. At sixteen Dempsey was already a thinking man, scrutinizing the world from behind his glasses.

The detective introduced himself and asked the boy if he believed Susan had any reason to run away.

"No, sir," Dempsey responded.

Dempsey stood in the evening shadows and coolly told the man he had no idea what had happened to Susan. On the Saturday morning of her disappearance he had seen her taking care of the two youngest Jacobson children. The detective commended the boy for helping out in the search and advised that he alone had the ability to play both sides of the street in order to obtain information.

"Know what I mean?" the investigator said, handing Dempsey his card.

"Both sides of the street," Dempsey repeated, smiling to himself.

That completed the only official interrogation of Dempsey. According to the family, in the next twenty-two months the Missing Persons Bureau called on the Jacobsons' only once: to retrieve Susan's dental chart.

Dorothy rose out of her seat like an angry phoenix coming to life.

"Come on, we've got work to do. We're going to the police department," she commanded.

The three got into Bob Allison's car. Driving to the station, down Jewett Avenue through Richmond Terrace, Ellen told Bob to make a right at a fork in the road.

"No," Dorothy said. "If we go the other way, to the left, we'll be heading in the correct direction. I get a very strong scent of oil. Very strong, as if I were in a barrel of oil."

Ellen thought nothing of the oil scent, as the entire area was surrounded by oil-producing companies and container companies. The police station was in the opposite direction, toward the Statue of Liberty, so Dorothy made a mental note of the direction and the trio proceeded to the station.

Carrying a red satchel, Dorothy followed Ellen and Bob into the Police Department where the nervous mother introduced herself to the patrolman on duty as the mother of Susan Jacobson, a missing child. No one knew what she was talking about. Then Dorothy asked to see one of the detectives.

The patrolman explained that if the case was being handled by missing persons, they could not interfere with the investigation. At that time the shift changed, and Dorothy caught two unsuspecting detectives walking in for duty.

She cornered them and briefly introduced herself, pulling out two large scrapbooks of affidavits and articles from cases she had resolved. Reluctantly they escorted her into an office where, behind closed doors, away from Ellen's ears, she told the two men that the case belonged in homicide, not missing persons. She told them that Susan Jacobson was not missing, she was dead, and that she had been murdered by someone who had known her for some time.

Seeing the policemen were skeptical, Dorothy began telling the officers details about other cases they were working on. She specifically talked about a man who was missing and who would be found in three days by the beach, or on something called "Beach," in an area known as Old Town. She predicted that the body would be found in the trunk of a large abandoned black car, like a Lincoln, with license plates that did not belong to the car. The car, she added, would not readily appear to have been abandoned.

The men agreed to go out with Dorothy, but their skepticism was a barrier to real cooperation. They drove around Staten Island for thirty minutes.

"We need facts, not psychics," the police told the Jacobsons, a response that would haunt the parents.

That evening Bill Jacobson listened to everything Dorothy said. Her descriptions seemed to fit various places he had visited in the past weeks.

Dorothy left the Jacobsons' house that evening sharing their sadness and frustration. She wondered whether, if the Jacobsons had been wealthy or if Susan had been the daughter of a policeman, they would have received different treatment.

Three days after Dorothy's first visit, the newspapers reported that a man's body had been found in an abandoned black Lincoln on Beach Street in the neighborhood known as New Dorp, a section of the island once known as Old Town. The dead man was "believed to be a New Jersey fisherman involved in organized crime narcotic trafficking."

The following week, on June 8, an article appeared on the front page of the Staten Island *Advance* announcing that the New Jersey psychic was working on the Jacobson case and that she had accurately predicted the discovery of the fisherman's body the week before. This illicited no response from the police.

Believing the police would do nothing with Dorothy's description of the pertinent area, Bill Jacobson continued to investigate on his own. Along with Gus Doyle and Bill's close friend, Dale Williams, Bill spent three days on the southern part of the island looking for the "MAR" Dorothy had described. On an island full of marine-related businesses, "MAR" would be three very common letters. But Dorothy's confidence and sympathy had lifted the spirits of the desperate parents. Bill Jacobson felt he would find everything Dorothy saw. By the time Dorothy returned the following weekend, the men had come up with a couple of possibilities.

Bill Jacobson invited the Staten Island reporter Janice Kabel to join them on the search with Dorothy. Although an invitation had been extended to the Missing Persons Bureau as well, no one from the Bureau showed up. So, the search party consisted of the parents, Dorothy, Dale Williams, and the reporter.

First the group went to a little wooded area near North Street, a street Dorothy had seen as important, and also near the water. As they walked down a dirt road in the summer heat, they looked through the trees and spotted an old trailer. The name on the van, which was partially blocked by the trees, began with "MAR." As they approached the van, however, the "MAR" became part of MARGOLIN Brothers. Dorothy walked around the area for a while, checking the van and the surrounding shrubbery, and finally said she picked up no feelings from it. Perhaps, she said, they would return to the spot at another time. She wanted to see the other location first.

In Mariner's Harbor they walked along a road, skirting rubbish piles, and into a dense area of vegetation where flies and mosquitoes buzzed around them mercilessly. In the distance tall cranes moved slowly in the air, looking like prehistoric creatures. They lifted their loads as if the tons of metal were weightless.

The area, known during World War I as Downey's Shipyard, had been used as docks for merchant ships. Huge concrete slabs, partially covered with plants and graffiti, and deep, dark caverns, which once had served as storage and water retainers, also gave the area the atmosphere of a spot once inhabited by an ancient civilization.

On a large concrete corner jutting out of the earth some fifteen feet, Bill pointed out red painted letters, probably the handiwork of kids leaving their mark. The letters spelled "MAR."

"This is it!" Dorothy's excitement was evident. Not thirty feet away from the slab was an abandoned junked car. "I know we're in the right place. I feel it all over me."

Looking south over a long concrete dividing wall, the

group could see the Bayonne Bridge and a train bridge spanning the bay. Across the water in New Jersey, two sets of dual steeples pointed heavenward.

But everywhere the earth was full of deep trenches and dark, forbidding holes, many containing dank water where insects were breeding in the summer heat. Dorothy shook her head, realizing the work involved in searching the underground network.

"You've got to get the police down here with bloodhounds and rowboats," Dorothy told them. "You must have their cooperation to get this investigation off the ground. I'm not a cop. I can point out where a person might be, but I can't go any further. That wouldn't stand up well in a courtroom," she advised Bill. "Your daughter is connected with this area and it's up to the police to find her."

The small, anxious man was overwhelmingly frustrated. Everytime he had turned to the police, he had encountered a blank wall. Only Dorothy's work had lifted his spirits. Only Dorothy continued to drive to Staten Island and spend time looking for their daughter. Dorothy would listen to their plight at any time, offering whatever solace and support she could.

But Ellen and Bill gave the information to the police, anyway. They were told, again, that the police "needed facts, not psychics." Moreover the police said they simply did not have the manpower to do the searching needed to cover the area Dorothy had pinpointed.

That evening, after the newspaper reporter had gone, Dorothy sat on Susan's bed with Ellen, feeling Susan's jewelry and thumbing through some photographs of the Jacobson children from a report Susan had done for school on her family life.

Dorothy looked at the photo of the attractive girl. Susan wore her long, light brown hair parted down the middle, framing her warm smile. She wore blue-tinted, wire-framed glasses, like her mother's, over her blue eyes.

Ellen sighed from exhaustion and sadness. Sitting quietly in Susan's room, she reflected on her daughter.

"She is so stubborn, sometimes," Ellen told Dorothy. "At nine months she was walking because she couldn't figure out how to crawl. She's smart, too. Almost straight A's in school."

The two mothers smiled.

"Stubbornness is in her planets," Dorothy said. "Ellen, I feel Susan had a bad time this last year. Is that right?"

Not exactly sure what Dorothy meant, Ellen asked her why she felt that way.

"Susan spent a lot of time with her boyfriend, didn't she?" Dorothy asked.

"I guess so." Ellen shrugged, not sure she wanted to pursue the sensitive subject. "We didn't really know how much time they were spending together," she said hesitantly. She wondered what Dorothy could be seeing. After all, Dorothy had not met Dempsey, yet.

"I feel they were doing a lot more than holding hands together," Dorothy continued, not sure how to pursue her feelings without offending the mother. But Ellen knew what the psychic was seeing.

"You're right, Dorothy, they were doing more than holding hands. Susan got pregnant and had to have an abortion last January." Tears streamed from the mother's eyes as she remembered the day the previous December, when she had found Susan in the bathroom, nauseated. Having had seven children, Ellen's subconscious suspicion was that her daughter was suffering from morning sickness. Unfortunately she had been correct.

What followed were several months of delicate textbook parenting. Without losing their equilibrium, Bill and Ellen helped their daughter through a difficult time with the support and understanding they knew she needed. She had made a mistake, but they didn't want her life ruined by it.

"This is the twentieth century," Ellen said to Dorothy. "It's no use hiding from these realities."

Susan's relationship with Dempsey had been slightly off-balance from the onset. They had met in grammar school and had played on the street in front of the Jacobsons' house on Anderson Avenue for more than a year without becoming close friends. Dempsey's confident and defensive air prevented anyone from seeing inside, from touching his vulnerabilities.

One day the previous August, while playing ball on the

street, Susan struck a direct emotional hit. Dempsey had been playing catcher, and the slender thirteen-year-old girl accidentally let go of the bat, which flew by Dempsey, striking his eye. He was rushed to the hospital where a doctor stitched up the bleeding eye in the emergency room. No visual damage had been done, but for weeks Dempsey strutted about with a patch over his eye.

Susan had been hysterical with grief. Her guilt and unhappiness gave way, eventually, to romance. As they entered school that September, they were one of the talked about "new romances." Dempsey, a freshman at Port Richmond High, and Susan, an eighth grader at Prall IS, West Brighton.

The emotional balance in their relationship never seemed to achieve an evenness. All along, Dempsey seemed to hold something over Susan. Trusting was difficult for Dempsey in a world that separated people by color. He didn't want to tread where he might be unwelcome, so one day he approached Susan's mother, Ellen.

"Do you object to me, Mrs. Jacobson?" the adolescent asked directly.

"Object to you?" Ellen repeated. "You mean am I prejudiced because you're not white and my daughter is? No," she stated flatly. "That doesn't really bother me. What does bother me," the concerned mother continued, "is the idea of a thirteen-year-old being seriously involved in a relationship. I don't mind you hanging around together on the street corners and playing, but I would prefer you didn't get too serious."

Dempsey became a fixture at the Jacobson house, coming and going as he pleased and sharing in Susan's family life. Ellen and Bill watched them play together that autumn within the familiar group on the street in front of their home. They sent them off to the movies with the other Jacobson children, riding either the bus or their bicycles, depending on the weather. Everyone seemed relaxed about the friendship.

Then, in November, came the parents' first inkling that something was awry. Susan brought home a report card with absences for which Ellen could not account. Her daughter insisted that she had helped Dempsey and his

188

family move on one day, and that on the second absence, she had waited around with Dempsey for the electrician and phone man to arrive.

After the abortion in late January Susan's parents insisted that the relationship terminate immediately. They were willing, however, to let Susan handle that situation in her own manner. For all her parents knew, Susan and Dempsey saw one another only occasionally, within their social group.

"I don't like what I hear," Dorothy said. "This boy gives me a lot of feelings. I think I need to see him. I wondered why I saw someone who wasn't black or white and sometimes both. Now I know. Has he been around lately?" Dorothy asked.

"All the time," Ellen said. "The evening Susan was missing I saw Dempsey on the corner. I asked him if he'd seen Susan and he said not since that morning. He had seen her in front of our house, taking care of my two youngest."

"He never talked to her that day?" Dorothy asked.

"That's right. From the second day on, he's been helping us search. He took two of my other kids around different areas looking for Susan. He's even reported ideas to us about where Susan might be." Despite her words, Ellen's voice revealed the suspicions she harbored toward Dempsey.

She remembered that after the abortion, in late February, the phone had begun ringing at odd hours, mostly after midnight. The anonymous caller would make threats against the Jacobsons' house. Ellen had recognized the voice as Dempsey's, but when she challenged him on the street, he had dispassionately denied being the caller.

Even after changing their number to an unlisted one, the calls persisted. This time Dempsey would get a friend to ask for Susan, and then would take the phone once Susan had answered.

Not long after that, in late February, Bill had been walking down the back steps one cold evening to put out the garbage. Susan had just left for a girl friend's house two blocks away, to go skating. Bill looked up the street and saw Dempsey walking with his cousin, Punky, toward the house where Susan was heading.

189

Bill ran back and retrieved his jacket, got into his car, and drove down Palmer Avenue. The two boys were walking no more than thirty feet behind his daughter. Bill drove up to Susan and told her to continue walking to her friend's, that he was going to talk with Dempsey.

Dempsey started throwing rocks at the car.

"Listen, Dempsey," Bill called out. "You want to know why we don't want you around anymore? You want to know why we don't want you with Susan? Get in the car and we'll talk about it like adults. I'll tell you what it's all about."

Dempsey started calling Bill names, but the man kept his composure, wanting to reason with the boy rather than quarrel. After a few minutes Dempsey got into the car and they drove for a bit until Bill parked the car on Jewett Avenue. He turned to the boy, who stared out the front window in silence.

Bill explained to the teen-ager that the reason Dempsey was unwelcome was because his daughter had been pregnant and had gone through an abortion. Dempsey's face showed no reaction; he said nothing more than "you're kidding."

Bill went on to say that he and Ellen didn't want either of the kids' lives destroyed by their ignorance, and that they felt it best to break off the relationship so that Susan and Dempsey could start fresh with other people.

"As far as I know, there are only four of us now who know about this," Bill said. "I suggest we go to your house now and tell your mother."

"I don't want to tell her now," Dempsey said. "I'll tell her later in my own way."

Bill relented and dropped the youth off in front of his mother's apartment.

Bill's sense of fairness was no deterrent to Dempsey's bitterness and anger. Now that the father had told him about Susan's abortion, the boy began spreading news of the incident, using the fact as a way to degrade Susan. The two continued to see one another, Susan often bearing the brunt of Dempsey's humiliating threats. Her stubbornness and pride, however, kept her from saying anything to her family.

In desperation the concerned parents tried again in April to reason with the two youngsters, having Dempsey to their home for dinner and discussing the subject openly, just as the textbooks prescribed. The evening seemed to go well, leaving Bill and Ellen hopeful that the situation was finally resolved.

On Saturday, May 15, the Jacobsons' house was full of goings-on; Ellen's parents had arrived from the Catskills. Bill and his father-in-law were remodeling the downstairs bathroom. Bill had taken out a loan to begin a major remodeling job on the four-decade-old house in which he had grown up. Born in 1939 of Swedish and German parents, Bill had raised his own children in the two-story house which had seen Jacobsons grow and die through the decades.

That bright Saturday morning, Ellen announced that dinner would be served at 5:30 and that she didn't want anyone to be late. With seven children and guests, experience told her it would be impossible to chase after anyone. Most of the time her children were usually on hand, anyway, playing in front of their house.

It wasn't till dinnertime that Susan was missed. Usually she would have been helping to set the table around 5:00. When that time came and she hadn't arrived, the family called out her name around the block a couple of times and, getting no response, sat down to eat.

Around 6:30 Ellen walked out front and called Susan again. She noticed Dempsey standing on the corner, so she headed in his direction.

"Hi, Dempsey," Ellen said. "Have you seen Susan around?"

"Haven't seen her since this morning, Mrs. Jacobson," he said politely, then got on his bicycle and rode away.

Soon after, the family split up and started looking for Susan. Telephones, bicycles, and cars were used for two hours as they tried to track her down.

One eleven-year-old reported having seen her in the early afternoon walking past the child's house. Susan had waved at the girl and said she was heading for Ralph's Ice Cream Parlor to see if she had a chance at getting a summer job. Someone else reported seeing her walking in the vicinity of Dempsey's apartment, but Dempsey had reported he hadn't been home. No one else remembered seeing her that afternoon.

Dorothy shook her head. She did not like the story Ellen told. The more she handled Susan's possessions, the more she felt Susan had been deeply troubled and frightened, and no one had known it. The pictures coming to Dorothy were not for discussion with the girl's parents. Ellen and Bill had been through enough, Dorothy felt.

In the days that followed their daughter's disappearance, Bill and Ellen watched the newspapers closely for reports of unidentified bodies found anywhere in the United States. As soon as they found something, such as a report of a discovered corpse or even part of a body, Ellen would send a dental chart and flier to the police department in the area. If only part of a body had been found, she would send a copy of an X-ray taken of Susan's spine months before she had disappeared, when it was discovered her spine had a slight curvature. But so far none of these efforts had uncovered news of Susan.

The last Saturday that June Dorothy invited Bill and Ellen to Nutley. She wanted Detective Lubertazzi to meet them and discuss possible ways they might go about the investigation.

The group spent a pleasant afternoon eating and drinking beer, talking about cases Dorothy had worked on with Lupo. Dorothy wanted to make the day relaxing for the Jacobsons, as both parents were showing signs of emotional stress.

It wasn't until dinnertime that Dorothy began asking questions about Dempsey. She wondered about his recent behavior toward them.

Bill informed her that Dempsey had been around constantly, having gone out on several searches with him, often for a whole afternoon. On different occasions Dempsey had taken Susan's sister Patricia searching in places he said he was suspicious of. The father admitted to having moments of suspicion, himself, when he looked at Dempsey because of the incidents of the past year. But he still believed Dempsey was not capable of doing anything really harmful to Susan.

Ellen agreed, although she admitted he had shown little or no remorse at Susan's disappearance.

"He just doesn't show much emotion at all," Ellen said as if defending him. She added that the boy had never once inquired into the Jacobson's own state of mind since their daughter's disappearance.

"I wonder," Dorothy said, "if he'd be willing to come here for a little talk. I'd like to talk with him," she told Bill.

"Sure. Why not? I'll call and see if anyone has seen him around. You do mean tonight, don't you?"

"Of course. I have another steak defrosted. Tell him I'll feed him," Dorothy said. "Kids like to eat. Some eat raw meat like lions, though," she said with an ominous smile at Lupo.

Bill called his home and Patricia reported that she had just seen Dempsey on the corner. When the boy got to the phone, Bill explained the situation and asked if Dempsey could come out to Nutley for a talk with Dorothy.

Dempsey agreed, and Bill persuaded a cousin to drive the teen-ager to a midpoint in New Jersey, where Bill met them, around 8:00 P.M.

By the time Dempsey arrived with Bill, Dorothy had cleared away the dishes from their dinner, and only one place was set in the corner for the late arrival. Dorothy had one steak on the grill for him, while the others sat around the table drinking coffee.

Dorothy had grave misgivings about Dempsey, and meeting him added fuel to her already heated feelings. She knew the Jacobsons were reluctant to point an accusing finger at the boy. She hoped to open them up to the fact that anyone, and everyone, should be suspected.

She looked into the boy's eyes and could sense his inner being. Here was a sixteen-year-old at the table with a cop, a psychic, and the parents of his former and missing girl friend. He was miles away from his own turf, yet he was in full control. Dempsey's self-supports were strong, she felt.

While feeding him, Dorothy showed Dempsey articles

about cases she had worked on with the police and the FBI. She showed him photographs of some of the missing children she had found.

"Do you believe in psychics?" Dorothy asked him.

"Guess so," he shrugged.

By now Dorothy did not trust Dempsey at all. Her instincts told her that he was capable of much more than Susan's parents would let themselves imagine.

"Dempsey, when did you see Susan that Saturday?" Dorothy asked as soon as the boy had finished eating.

"That morning. She was taking care of the two little kids," he told her.

"So that was the only time you saw her that day. Correct?"

"That's what I said."

"How many times did you go home that day?" Dorothy asked him.

"I didn't go back till after I saw the Jacobsons and she asked if I'd seen Susan," he said, indicating Ellen.

"So you never went home till that evening?"

"Right."

"How come I see you in two different shirts that day? I see you in a red and black striped shirt. Like a sweater shirt."

"You mean my hockey shirt? Yeah, I was wearing that shirt that day."

"You weren't wearing that shirt in the afternoon," Dorothy stated.

Dempsey thought for a moment, never averting his eyes.

"I guess I did go home early that afternoon. That shirt was too hot. I forgot about that," he said without batting an eye.

"About what time? Just after lunch?" Dorothy guessed.

"Yeah, I guess around that time," Dempsey agreed, this time hesitantly.

Bill and Ellen were surprised by the news. For four weeks Dempsey had said he had not been home that afternoon. Now it turned out he had been home about the time Susan had been seen heading in the general direction of his house—about 1:30 that afternoon.

"Big deal. So I forgot a little thing," he said, sensing the tension in the air.

"It is a big deal," Dorothy said to him.

"I can't believe you lied like that," Ellen said quietly, her voice quivering.

"Dempsey, what was your relationship with Susan like?" Dorothy resumed her questioning.

Dempsey shrugged.

"I don't know what that means," Dorothy pursued.

"Not too terrific," he finally said.

"What do you mean, not too terrific? I thought you two were in love," Dorothy said.

"What love?" he said. "We just screwed a lot."

"You son of a bitch!" Bill slammed his fist on the table. "One minute you love her, the next you make her a piece of meat. You're a sick bastard, Dempsey."

As if not hearing the father's words, Dempsey went on.

"We screwed because she thought she was a lezzie," he said flatly. "She thought I was good looking and could help . . ." Before he could finish, Ellen rose and left the room, followed shortly by Bill, who glared into Dempsey's face. Words stuck in the father's throat as he struggled with anger and hurt. Lupo looked at Dorothy, knowing full well where she was heading. He got up and turned to the door.

"I'll make sure they're okay," he said, leaving the room.

As soon as the two were alone, Dorothy leaned over the table, pinning the boy into the corner. She kept her full weight on the table, leaning forward, grabbing his shirt collar.

"What is this crap you're telling me, Dempsey? I don't go for any of it. You have no decency as a human being, saying those things in front of people who've been much too kind to you." Dorothy twisted his shirt in anger.

Dempsey's eyes were wide, his breathing fast and nervous.

"I would never have been nice to you, like they've been. Never. Especially if you'd done the things you did to that girl and she was my daughter. I'd have your throat in a minute," she challenged him.

"I don't know what you're talking about, lady," Dempsey began. "I only slapped her face."

"You know exactly what I'm talking about. You took that girl to Mariner's Harbor and did her in. You did, didn't you?"

Dempsey was speechless. Their eyes held each other as Dorothy released her grip but still leaned against the table. Dempsey averted his gaze.

"You're lucky I'm not a cop," Dorothy told him. "You don't have to say a thing, of course. But I know you killed her. My knowing won't do any good, I'm afraid. The police will have to find out for themselves."

Dorothy thought of the investigation so far and felt furiously frustrated.

"I didn't kill her. I didn't do it," Dempsey insisted, his voice holding back the rage and fear he was feeling.

"I got all I wanted tonight." Dorothy moved away from the table and sighed. "Now, can I give you another piece of cake?" She smiled wryly at Dempsey and left the room.

Dorothy was exhausted. It was after 1:00 A.M. Ellen had been resting on the couch for the duration of Dorothy's interrogation, while Lupo and Bill went over facts and possibilities on the case.

Dorothy opened the kitchen door, entering the den like a doctor coming out of the delivery room into a waiting room full of expectant families. She slapped her hands together in a "job-well-done" fashion and announced that she was tired and ready to kick everyone out for the night.

Bill went into the kitchen and told Dempsey they were ready to return to Staten Island. At this point Bill was still unsure of Dempsey. The Jacobsons were not aware of the depth of Dorothy's strong feelings about the youth. But Dempsey had lied, and the parents could not help but feel more suspicious.

Dorothy abided by her cardinal rule of never telling a missing child's parents that she knew the child was dead. Therefore she could not reveal all her feelings about Dempsey to the Jacobsons. Dorothy knew, too, that for the Jacobsons to accuse Dempsey would get them nowhere, so she suggested to Bill and Ellen that Dempsey be given a polygraph. Polygraphs were not very reliable, but she hoped the fear of taking the polygraph would push him to talk.

Gus Doyle, who was still helping the Jacobsons, agreed that the polygraph would be a good idea, and he volunteered to make the arrangements for the examination in Manhattan. Written permission was obtained from Dempsey's mother, who had had no contact at all with the Jacobsons before or since Susan's disappearance. Bill Jacobson paid the $200 for the examination. By now most of his home-improvement loan had been eaten away by the costs of the investigation.

It was the first week in July that Dempsey went to Manhattan for the polygraph. When he was asked by the polygraph examiner if he had murdered Susan, he stated his innocence. The machine registered that he was telling the truth. Nevertheless he revealed facts to the interrogator that he had not disclosed to the Jacobsons.

As soon as the test was completed, Dempsey called Gus Doyle. He admitted that he had seen Susan the Saturday she disappeared. In fact, he said, she had been at his apartment after lunch, where they had had an argument.

"She left crying," Dempsey told Gus. "I never saw her again." And the teen-ager hung up.

Gus knew that Dempsey had not been seen on the street that Saturday till 4:00 P.M. Between 1:30 and 4:00 he had no reliable alibi and claimed to have been alone.

When Bill and Ellen heard from Gus that Dempsey had passed the polygraph, but not without divulging some interesting new facts, they could only think that Dorothy's intuition about the boy had been right. After six weeks Dempsey admitted not only to having gone home to change shirts but also to having been with Susan in his own apartment.

Bill saw Dempsey on the street the next day and invited him upstairs for a talk. Bill had drawn a map of the area, detailing it with the places Susan was reported to have passed or possibly visited that Saturday afternoon. In light of Dempsey's recent admission, the map forced suspicion on him.

"You kept telling us you hadn't seen Susan that day."

Bill looked hard at the teen-ager. "Then you told Dorothy you did go home, but just to change your shirt. That was around lunchtime. That's about the time Susan was last seen."

Bill was anxious, sitting there with Dempsey. He felt angrier than he had been in a long time. Dempsey was taller and more athletic than Bill, but the father wanted the truth, and he would use physical force if necessary.

"If you look at this map, it's hard not to place the blame on you," Bill said.

Dempsey looked directly into Bill's eyes, as if challenging him.

"Well then, you'll have to prove it," Dempsey said sarcastically.

Bill lunged forward and grabbed Dempsey's shirt. Flying back in fear, Dempsey landed against the kitchen counter. He took hold of the kitchen chair and threw it at Bill, shattering glasses in its path. Dempsey dived for the door and ran down the narrow steps. Out front he picked up a large rock and hurled it at the Jacobsons' front door, smashing it, then ran up the street and was gone.

If ever guilt was evident, Bill felt, it was in Dempsey's behavior. How much more certain could he be that Dempsey was responsible for his daughter's disappearance?

Bill went to Dempsey's mother's house that evening, looking for the boy. Dempsey had not been home since their encounter. The well-dressed, attractive mother sat and listened to Bill's story and his obvious concern with her son. After he had been there more than an hour, the phone rang. It was Dempsey.

Bill listened as Mrs. Hawkins pleaded with her son to come home and discuss the matter. Dempsey argued that his mother did not love him, that no one really cared for him, and that his problems were her fault.

"What do you mean, I don't love you?" Bill heard the anxious mother say as she paced back and forth in the small, dark hallway.

"You're not talking sense. Commit suicide? Dempsey, come home and talk to me. You'll be safe here, I promise you. No one is going to do anything to you."

The tall, dark-haired woman put the phone down and

shook her head. She turned to Bill and sighed, looking confused and without real direction. Bill soon departed, leaving the mother to await the arrival of her son.

The next day Dempsey was hanging out on the corner as usual. This time, however, he paid no attention to the Jacobson house. Nor did the Jacobsons attempt communication. Bill and Ellen were too angry and hurt to talk with Dempsey again.

But the boy's presence was always felt. He and some friends took to showing up on the corner with radios blaring at night, often as late as 2:00 A.M. The angry parents decided to ignore, as much as possible, his juvenile behavior.

Dorothy and Lupo felt something had to be done about getting Dempsey interrogated again by the police. The polygraph had proven both positive and negative; though he had passed it, it had brought out new evidence that could only bring him closer to being incriminated.

Lupo called the Missing Persons Bureau and informed them that he and Dorothy both felt Dempsey was guilty. The detective he spoke with said that he had already interrogated the boy and felt he was not only innocent, but a help in getting information about the girl's whereabouts. That a psychic felt Susan had not run away proved nothing to the officials involved.

By August Bill was usually searching alone after work, although he was sometimes aided by friends or Dorothy. Dempsey's face was seen less and less as he involved himself with other neighborhood friends and stayed away from the Jacobson house. Dorothy's feelings never wavered, nor did her vision of where Susan's body would be found.

It wasn't until November that Dorothy underwent hypnosis with Dr. Ribner. Bill had asked that someone from the Missing Persons Bureau be present, and had been told the Bureau would cooperate. The group waited for someone from the Bureau to arrive, and then, after forty-five minutes, went on without him. Bill had brought along his own cassette recorder.

Dr. Ribner asked Bill to wait outside during the first

199

session. He explained that a family member's emotions could prevent Dorothy from seeing clearly. Bill consented.

Gus Doyle and Dr. Ribner proceeded to interrogate the psychic. In that first of two sessions, Dorothy told them that she saw Susan, and that the girl had been strangled to death. The murderer was black, she said, and everyone in the family knew him. Once again she described the area she had originally seen around Mariner's Harbor. "Susan is in water, but she didn't drown," Dorothy said. "I smell oil. Very strong oil odor, as if I could suffocate from it."

She also told them she saw another body that was not Susan Jacobson's, but that would be found in the Richmond Town area within the next two days. The body was that of a woman who had been dead several days.

When Gus played the tape that night for Bill and Ellen, it was the first verbal confirmation they had from Dorothy that their daughter was dead. In the six months they had worked with her, not once had she openly stated to them that Susan had been murdered. They found themselves crying, even though they had felt all along that Susan could not be alive.

The next day a woman's corpse was found in Richmond Town in the manner Dorothy had foreseen. Bill and Ellen were excited, hoping to provide substantiation to the police of Dorothy's abilities.

The couple was even more determined to prove her abilities publicly after Dorothy's second session with Ribner, during which she described in detail a scene in which another body would be found on Staten Island within days. This time she mentioned a cemetery and something she saw on a hill.

"Isn't it funny," she said, "that I see a lighthouse on land? Can that be? It's not close to the water."

She went on to describe a nearby golf course and an area known as Toad Hill. She said the woman's body, which had already been buried once and dug up again, would be found near the lighthouse.

"It's not Susan, though," Dorothy cautioned.

"Dorothy, try and get back to Susan," Dr. Ribner guided her. "See what's around Susan."

Dorothy was quiet for a moment while she focused again. This time, however, she did not get the scene in Mariner's Harbor.

"I see horses. Several horses running along a trail. I'm getting something like silver, too. I'm not sure it's the metal I feel or just the word. Or a word close to it. Now, somewhere near those horses I see a gravestone. One of those large, family-type stones. Wait, I'm getting a name on it." She hesitated for a moment while Bill Jacobson, sitting next to the tape recorder, watched her work through inexplicable mental channels.

"The name I see on the gravestone is John and Mary Moore," Dorothy reported. She also gave the dates inscribed on the stone, and described a long plank of wood over which people would cross.

Bill was excited by the details. This time he and Ellen wanted to prove to the police that Dorothy was on target. For the next several days they searched through cemeteries for the names John and Mary Moore. Since it was a common name, plenty of Moores were found, but none with the right first names. Every Staten Island cemetery was searched, but they came up with nothing.

At the same time they searched for the "lighthouse" Dorothy had seen. The Jacobsons wanted to find the body of the woman Dorothy had seen and lead the police to it. But they were beaten to the finish by two little boys who discovered the woman's body behind a round, turn-of-the-century home that resembled a turreted old English home. In Dorothy's eyes the tall, round structure resembled a lighthouse.

The months seemed to pass in a cloud of sadness for the Jacobson family. Winter had set in, and the searching came to a standstill. The only important development was that Dempsey had left school that January. Fellow students reported to the Jacobsons that their daughter's former boyfriend had left Staten Island. Rumor had it he was somewhere in the Midwest.

The rumors were correct. Dempsey had gone to live with his father, a farmer, in a little rural town in Illinois, called Joppa, population 500. As far as the Jacobsons knew, Dempsey had never even met his father; now he was living with him.

With Dempsey out of reach and the police investigation at a standstill, there seemed no hope of ever finding Susan.

Dorothy, wherever she traveled, kept Susan's picture with her. While in Baltimore in March, 1977, Dorothy checked the police department to see if Susan was listed on the national missing-persons printout. She discovered that her name had never appeared on the national list, only on the New York State file which was located in Albany.

On Tuesday, March 14, 1978, Dorothy sat in her den with three detectives from the Missing Persons Bureau of the Bergen County Police Department. On March 1, Detective Rufino had called Dorothy concerning a missing youth the police were having trouble locating. Rufino felt the nineteen-year-old boy had run into problems but was stumped as far as clues were concerned. Rufino brought two fellow detectives with him, Charlie Serwin and Tony Tortora.

While they were discussing the case, Rufino was called away by his department on an emergency. As the men had traveled in two cars, Tortora and Serwin wondered if Dorothy might be willing to help them on three other cases whose files they had brought with them. The three separate cases all involved teen-agers, and none had been resolved by conventional means. Virtually no clues existed. Two cases dated back a year, one was only sixty days old.

Dorothy agreed to see if one of the cases might strike a chord in her which would help them. She sat on her couch, legs crossed, cigarette in hand, trying to focus on a vision she had of someone who might be one of the teen-agers involved. She had a feeling that the boy she had in mind was known to the detectives, although possibly his was not one of the cases on hand. She was having trouble getting details, though.

As Dorothy and the men discussed the missing teen-agers, a drama began to open in her vision.

Three boys were moving about together in a vast, empty area, as if scrambling for something. Swamplike, the area was bordered by a highway on one side. She could also see a car. Then she saw another boy, but he was on the ground and still. Finally she saw a knife.

"I'm getting something with a stabbing," she interrupted them. "But I don't think it's one of the kids you're looking for today."

"We're not here for a stabbing," Tortora said. "We're not homicide. As far as we're concerned, these kids are just missing. We have no real grounds for suspecting foul play."

"You don't call 'missing' foul play?" Dorothy asked. "If my kid was missing, the first thing I'd smell would be foul play."

"These kids may have split on their own," Serwin offered. "We were hoping you'd be able to help us with that."

"I don't care," Dorothy said. "I see what I see, and I think one of you knows about this stabbing."

The men looked at one another, perplexed and wondering how to gain control of the situation. Dorothy went on with her vision.

She told them she saw three boys around the age of nineteen or twenty, in a large field, and that she had the feeling the field was located behind an airport, or some place to do with airplanes.

Next she described a wall. She said the area was known as the "wall," and that kids came to that area to gather and drink at night. She felt the "wall" was part of an old building that had been destroyed by fire and was near water.

Dorothy got up and pulled a clean piece of paper out of a drawer in the bookcase. She began to draw what she was seeing. Tortora watched the rustic map evolve of a place Dorothy had never visited. After a few minutes the two detectives decided the map resembled the area around the Passaic Avenue bridge across the Saddle River in Lodi.

"It isn't near the airport," she said, handing the map to Tortora. "There's an empty lot adjacent to it that'll soon have a building built on it. Something official, like a courthouse." She stopped for a moment, focusing on the area around the "wall." "There's a building nearby that has the word 'water' written on it. Water is part of the name of the building, I think."

Tortora and Serwin sat in amazement. They had no idea what to do with the facts; only Tortora was beginning to recognize landmarks.

"Did this guy drown?" Tortora asked.

"No, I'd know that for sure. This boy was stabbed to death and buried in dirt. I know one of you is aware of this case," she told them.

"Can you describe the kid at all?"

"I get a boy in his late teens. Good looking, with glasses. Very strong. A fighter in strength, but not necessarily in temperament. I see him very active in sports."

Tortora thought about Dorothy's decription for a few minutes before saying anything. He did have a case, he told her, dating back to late September, concerning a seventeen-year-old Lodi boy who had never been found. As soon as he began telling Dorothy about the boy, she felt they were on the same track.

"The kid's mother has been trying to get in touch with you for six months now," he informed her. "She called and wrote the Nutley Police Department, and they told her they would forward her name to you when you weren't busy on other cases. That was last October."

Dorothy flinched, thinking of the hundreds of letters and phone calls Lupo and Phyllis had to field. The thought of the desperate mothers turning to her for help depressed her.

"Call her now," Dorothy said. "Tell her to come over."

Nancy Locascio was thrilled to hear that Dorothy Allison would work on her son's disappearance. The call from the Bergen detective lifted her out of her despondency. The short, dark-haired woman had been to the threshold of insanity in her desperate six-month search for her son, Ronnie, the third of her four children.

Ronnie Stica had been missing since early evening, September 22, 1977. The good-looking, sandy-haired youth had no reason to run away, as the police had suggested.

A junior, Ronnie had dropped out of high school the previous year with his mother's approval, having opted for a period of work and earning money. The youth was a great collector, having amassed a sizable coin collection and "newspaper firsts" collection.

Ronnie was an athlete, a body builder, and a star pitcher; his room full of trophies and plaques attested to his abilities as a player. Though not a great student, he realized that school was not everything, that education could be attained through other means.

Nancy's four children, Susan, Joey, Ronnie, and thirteen-year-old Bobby, had been close to one another in a way Nancy had never been able to experience in her own youth. Nancy spent her very early years in Brooklyn's Italian and Jewish neighborhoods with her parents, her twin brother, and her sister. Both parents died within a year of one another in 1942, leaving the children alone and without means.

Nancy had been adopted by an Italian family in Lodi, New Jersey, a quiet, northern New Jersey town that is still predominantly Italian. She had been separated from her siblings, who were taken in by relatives.

Nancy met her first husband, Leon Stica, in high school and married him after graduation when he became a policeman in the Bergen County Police Department.

Life had been difficult for her; her emotional foundation was not always able to support her in times of stress. Although she wrestled with marital problems and eventually a divorce, her children remained close and loving—until Ronnie was discovered missing that warm fall evening.

Ronnie had been expecting potential buyers to come around and inspect his car late that evening; he hoped to sell it before he and his sister, Susan, entered night school that October to get their diplomas. Afraid to damage the car, he chose not to drive it at all.

When Nancy got home from her job at a nearby department store where she was a clerk, Susan, who lived with her husband, Johnny, downstairs in the white wooden house, asked Nancy if she might borrow her mother's car to run some errands. Ronnie made the same pitch almost simultaneously, wanting to meet some friends at De Vries Park, a housing development, for an hour. Susan agreed to drop Ronnie off and go about her business.

205

"It would be terrible," Nancy lamented in jest, "if my children ever had to walk anyplace. God forbid you should have to walk two blocks." She recalled the time Ronnie had taken a cab home without the funds for the fare, leaving Nancy to pay.

Susan and Ronnie drove to De Vries Park, chatting and joking with one another. Ronnie said he was to meet some "buddies" for a while and then he'd grab a lift home, or call his brother Joey for a ride if Susan was still out with the car.

Tall and well built, Ronnie struggled out of the small yellow Firebird, finding relief in stretching his legs again. Susan watched him walk toward a fellow she recognized as a recent acquaintance of his, a local boy named Dave Menicola. The athletic-looking boy nodded at Ronnie, and Susan drove off, having seen her brother alive for the last time.

At home Nancy was tired. The department store had been undergoing renovation, forcing the staff to work twice as hard, leaving her exhausted. She crawled into bed early that night.

The next morning Nancy noticed Ronnie wan't around, and she assumed he had stayed the night at his girl friend Carol's house. Nancy liked Carol and was glad her son had found himself a positive relationship.

It wasn't until Nancy returned home from work that evening that she got word that something was awry. The phone rang and it was Carol, looking for Ronnie.

"Didn't he stay with you last night?" she asked.

"No. I haven't seen him at all," the girl friend said. "I was wondering why he hadn't called."

Nancy had a sickening feeling in the pit of her stomach. She immediately began calling relatives and friends, trying to place Ronnie.

No one had seen him. As a mother's instant fears pervaded her consciousness, Nancy, dizzy and nauseous, had to sit down. Ronnie was a strong boy, she told herself, so it was unlikely that he had gotten into any serious trouble. Unless he had hurt someone and was too frightened to tell her.

After several hours of calling and searching, the weakened mother got into her car and drove to the Lodi Police Department. With tears streaming down her face, she told a policeman that her seventeen-year-old son had been out all night and had not been heard from since the previous day.

The policeman said that teen-agers had a habit of getting into trouble and forgetting about their parents.

"I wouldn't worry too much," he told her. "Sons have a way of finding their way home."

"Ronnie always calls," Nancy insisted. "Even when he's going to be a half hour late, he calls."

The policeman took down her name but asked very few questions. Nancy was frustrated and angry, feeling the police weren't going to do anything. The volatile woman stormed out of the station, as she would do again, several times, in the following months.

Nancy had tried to reach Dave Menicola whom she had never met but had heard about from Ronnie and Susan. The woman who answered the Menicola phone told Nancy in broken English that she was Dave's grandmother, and that Dave was not around. He was in the hospital.

"Why is he in the hopital?" Nancy gasped, frightened to hear this response.

"I don't know, they don't tell me anything. They think I'm stupid," the pitiful-sounding woman said.

"Which hospital is he in?" Nancy asked.

"I don't know," came the woman's reply. "They think I'm too stupid to be told these things."

Exasperated, Nancy slammed the phone down and reached for the directory in search of hospital numbers. It took awhile before she tracked down Dave Menicola at Hackensack Hospital.

All the while, Nancy's mind raced with frightening possibilities. Could Ronnie have injured this boy, sending him to the hospital? Not Ronnie . . . It just didn't seem possible.

She finally had the twenty-year-old Menicola on the phone.

He told Nancy he had been to a party the night before and had accidentally cut himself on a broken bottle.

207

"Where was Ronnie?" she asked.

"I don't know. He didn't go to the party. He headed over to the wall, last I saw him."

"To the wall? How did he get there?" Nancy pursued, dragging on a cigarette.

"Walking. I guess he walked," Menicola said.

"Walked? Ronnie walked to the wall?" came the incredulous reply. "Ronnie would never walk anywhere," Nancy told the boy, "much less to the wall. He'd take a taxi first."

Nancy didn't like the sound of the boy's voice. Too steady, she thought. Too cool. He had his story comfortably in his head. Something told her he was not telling the truth.

Nancy went to the police station and told them what she had discovered. She explained that Menicola was the last person known to have been with Ronnie, and now he claimed not to know where Ronnie had been the previous night. She entreated them to check with Hackensack Hospital and make certain that Menicola's story was on the level. The police said that there was no law against lying, and if the kid was in the hospital, they couldn't just check up on a patient without substantial reason.

The next day Nancy found out where the supposed party had been held, and that night she called the people whose house it had been held in. She explained who she was and wondered if they knew David Menicola had hurt his arm.

The woman who answered said there had been no party at their house that they knew of, and if one of their son's friends had cut his arm and been taken to a hospital during an incident in their home, they would certainly have known about it.

Nancy, driven to distraction by the police's insistence that Ronnie had run away and would return shortly like the thousands of other kids reported missing, went back to the detective who had been assigned to the case and told him about the party and the lies.

The man carefully took down everything Nancy reported, and said the police would investigate in the usual manner.

"Everything will get checked," he assured her.

In the meantime Nancy's life had reached a tragic low. She struggled to work, she cared little about herself, she found herself snapping at people uncontrollably. Susan, Joey, and Bobby were with her as much as possible, trying everything possible to find Ronnie. Instead of familiar banter and joking, silence permeated their family life, and stayed like an uncomfortable guest.

Nancy had a recurring dream for the first several weeks after Ronnie's disappearance. Three teen-aged boys, all without faces, stood around a body which lay quietly on the ground. That body was Ronnie's, Nancy knew, and they were burying him.

Nancy called relatives out of state, just in case Ronnie might be traveling across country. Two cousins were law-enforcement officers and they checked their own departments for information. They informed Nancy that Ronnie's name was not yet listed on the national missing-persons list.

She went to the Lodi police and broke into the captain's office.

"I won't leave here until I find out what is happening with my son," she demanded. "I won't leave till I'm sure you're doing something."

The captain tried to calm her down.

"Did you ever put out a missing-person alarm on Ronnie?" she inquired.

The captain replied affirmatively.

"I want to see a copy of the bulletin," she demanded.

Nancy sat and waited in the small smoke-filled office for twenty minutes until the captain returned.

"I'm sorry, Mrs. Locascio, we can't find the copy of the report. It must have been misplaced in the files."

"I know why you can't find it." Nancy rose and challenged the slow-moving official. "It's because you never did it. You bastards never put it through," she screamed.

Despite the official's assurances, Nancy continued to believe her son's name had not been put on the national list.

Nancy went to Chief Andy Voto's office next and demanded that he telephone Dave Menicola while she stood in his office. He agreed to call and talk with the boy if

209

Nancy would sit quietly. He didn't want her to speak with him.

Voto called Menicola and after thirty minutes of exasperating discussion with Dave and his frightened mother, he got them to agree to a brief interrogation in his office.

Roughly handsome and of medium height, Menicola seemed more nervous of his anxious mother and the mood emanating from Nancy than he was of the officer's questions. He told the chief that he had cut his arm on a piece of glass. It wasn't exactly a formal party he'd gone to, he explained; he was just messing around with some buddies. One of them took him to Hackensack Hospital where the attending doctor said he'd have to spend the night due to the extent of the cut. While he talked, his mother sat on the edge of her seat, chain-smoking, as if ready to leap to her son's defense.

Voto finished his questioning and accepted the story, thanking the pair for their cooperation.

All along Nancy had wanted more help than she felt the police would provide. Next she wrote the Internal Revenue district offices in several states, explaining in her letter that her son was missing and that she realized, due to the Privacy Act, they could not tell her directly if Ronnie was in their area. Nevertheless she sent along a letter that could be forwarded to him, if he could be located. The letter read:

December 24, 1977
My Darling Ronnie,
It's been 3 months now since we have seen or heard from you. We don't know if you are dead or alive. I'm afraid something awful has happened to you. If you are alive and you do get this letter, please, Ronnie, get in touch with us. We are desperate to find you. My hand is shaking so badly I can hardly write. We have had two detectives looking for you for some time now. We are putting your picture on TV and posting a $1,000.00 reward for your whereabouts. Please, please, Ronnie, if you are reading this, contact us in some way. We love you so much and we want to know where you are. I can't make myself believe you just

210

ran away and left all your possessions behind. Tomorrow is Christmas and next week is your birthday, but it won't be the same without you.

Ronnie, I love you so much. My life is so empty. Please take the pain away from my heart.

I love you.

Mommy, Daddy, Joey, Susan, Bobby, Johnny, Suzanne, Baby Joey, John and baby Sue, Uncle Tom and everyone in town is praying to know you're well.

Copies of the letter were sent across the country. Nancy paid to have Ronnie's picture put into newspapers and had to handle the appeals as paid advertising.

At the same time Nancy had gone to tea-leaf readers, psychics, palm and tarot card readers. She attended psychic fairs where practitioners would give her bits of information at $5–$10 a hit.

Each time Nancy would hear a different description of her son's location and situation, she would go home and cry. One psychic told her Ronnie was in the Nevada desert, having been taken there by a motorcycle gang and was wrapped in a yellow-flowered blanket. Another said he was in a commune in Ohio. Yet another said he was in a nearby cemetery, in a crypt with a broken lock.

Nancy and her kids searched the Lodi cemeteries for a crypt with a broken lock. Crypts with gates ajar were found, but most were open due to the extreme cold and heavy snows. Nothing was found after two days of cold searching.

In scanning the papers daily, Nancy would respond to any item that reported the finding of a body. One day she found an article that said a large box wrapped in Christmas foil had been found with a body inside, but the corpse had been cut into six-inch slices. What most alarmed Nancy was the fact that the box was found at the end of her ex-husband's street. After two days of calls and worries, Nancy was told the body was that of a woman who had been a prostitute.

Nancy had read about Dorothy Allison in the *National Enquirer* and tried to reach her in nearby Nutley. She had called Detective Lubertazzi at the Nutley Police Department and was told that Dorothy was overbooked and working on several cases at the time. Detective Tortora of the Bergen County police said he had met Dorothy and would try to bring the two women together.

When Tony Tortora called from Dorothy's house, Nancy had an intuitive feeling that important things were about to happen. She remembered seeing Dorothy's photograph in the papers and believed the woman to be sincere, unlike some of the other psychics she had dealt with. At the very least, they were *paesans*.

Nancy and Joey, her twenty-year-old son and an aspiring musician and lyricist, drove to Nutley. Dorothy greeted Nancy warmly, giving her instant encouragement and solace. Nancy was grateful to Dorothy for her strong support and came to rely on her from that moment on. Dorothy quickly became part of Nancy's family and life.

Nancy, Joey, and the two detectives sat around the kitchen table while Dorothy went to work on Ronnie Stica.

"Do you know anyone with a pilot's license? Or an airplane?" Dorothy asked.

"No," Nancy said.

"No one that flies a plane or spends time at airports for some reason?" Dorothy questioned.

"No one in my family has anything to do with planes," Nancy said.

"Ralph. I get the name Ralph. Anyone you know?"

Nancy and Joey tried to think of a "Ralph" they knew, but could not.

Nancy had brought a pair of Ronnie's glasses with her, so that Dorothy could hold something he had worn. After she held the pilot's glasses for a while, she put them down on the Formica table and began pursuing other images.

"Nancy, I see a yellow building. Ronnie had something to do with that building. Let me see what more I can tell you. It has the word 'water' on it."

Nancy remembered that the building where Susan had dropped Ronnie was several stories high and was a pale yellow color. She had no idea where the word "water" came from.

"I see a yellow car with a black roof," Dorothy continued. Nancy recognized that as her own Firebird, the car in which Susan and Ronnie had driven.

It was when Dorothy began to speak of the "wall" that Nancy felt she had at last found a true psychic. Everything Dorothy said fit the description of the infamous "wall" where the kids hung out, smoking and drinking. It was a large retaining wall alongside a part of the Passaic River, and Dorothy saw it as if she had been there.

Dorothy could see from Nancy's excitement that she was close to the reality of the situation. She wanted to get up and go to Lodi, but the detectives had other appointments. Nancy agreed to drive around with Dorothy that next Sunday, which was Palm Sunday.

As they were saying good-bye, Dorothy told Tortora privately to look for a piece of a blue car in the vacant area behind the airport.

"Something fell off the car," she told him. "That blue car is important. Ronnie was in that car that night."

She also told him to look for anything with the word "eclipse," either a street sign or an advertisement. She felt Ronnie's body was not too far from the "eclipse."

Seeing how emotionally overwrought Nancy was, Dorothy told her that she would not, could not work with anyone so volatile. Dorothy's emotions and her psychic power were too closely connected, she explained, and would be blurred by a mother's emotions. It was partly for that reason that Dorothy never told parents if she saw their child dead, or took them to the victim's grave. Dorothy also knew the law about tampering with a corpse, possibly contaminating it and ruining the evidence.

Meeting Dorothy and sensing her confidence and sympathy infused Nancy with new hope: hope in which she wanted desperately to believe. For six months she had listened to detectives and psychics theorize or shrug their shoulders, and for six months hardly a night had passed that she had not shed tears. The police had even suggested that her own son, Joey, was not beyond suspicion. But when the angry family insisted on his taking a polygraph, the police had refused to administer it.

That night Nancy felt stronger and more positive than she had felt in months. That night Nancy did not cry.

The following day Dorothy drove to the Lodi police station and met the two dectectives. They sat for a few minutes discussing aspects of the case that Dorothy had sensed during the night. Meeting Nancy had sent her into a whirlwind of feelings and visions. Dorothy's instant warmth and sympathy for the woman and her suffering made her want to resolve the case quickly. She knew she could.

Tortora had taken some time after work the previous day to search around Teterboro Airport. He admitted it was difficult trying to pick one spot in which to search in such a large area. But he had found one interesting item: the skirt from a blue car, which was a recent model.

Dorothy was pleased, sensing immediately that they were on the right track.

"Let's start driving around. I don't want to get in the car with Nancy on Sunday and take her to her son's body. She doesn't need that."

They drove for almost two hours, but they stayed within Lodi, rather than driving to the airport. Dorothy first asked to be taken to a street or place that would have some connection to the telephone company. She had no feelings about the actual telephone company building when they passed it, so Tortora suggested "Bell Avenue."

"That's it," Dorothy said. "Someone who lives on Bell Avenue gives me very strong feelings."

They drove down the tree-lined street of older homes. Dorothy indicated that one of the perpetrators, "one of the animals," lived on that street.

Tortora and Serwin did not tell Dorothy that Dave Menicola lived on the block she pinpointed; they simply took note of the fact and continued driving.

Next they drove to DeVries Park. They walked around the area where Ronnie had been left by his sister, and Dorothy felt his presence as she had seen it in her mind. She could picture his getting out of the yellow and black car and meeting his "buddy."

"I think these kids were up to something," she told the detectives. "They didn't just kill him. One of them thought they had good reason to do him in. Poor Nancy, she should know."

214

It wasn't until Palm Sunday that Dorothy finally got to Teterboro Airport. Nancy and her son-in-law, Johnny, drove Dorothy around DeVries Park first. Dorothy was trying to follow the path the boys had taken the night of September 22.

Nancy and Dorothy walked around the yellow building. Walking through the small dirt playground alongside the building, where mothers and their children were playing, Dorothy noted that part of the original name of the building was still in evidence. What remained of "Water Works Building" was only the first word.

Next they drove to Teterboro. Dorothy remembered the two businessmen who had been heading for Teterboro four years before and whose plane had crashed in southern New Jersey. She was finally seeing their destination, a busy, small private airport.

In a vast, swampy area behind the airport Dorothy walked with her companions. As soon as she had spent some time walking around on the cool, sunny day, she felt certain that Ronnie was in the area. Tortora had told her where to find the blue skirt, but she didn't want Nancy to accidentally trip over her son's leg.

Nancy walked alone, her head down, her eyes fixed on anything that might have been a grave. She picked up a broken white vase. She thought it was a beautiful piece of ceramic, and an odd item to find in such a desolate area.

While she stood musing, Dorothy quietly told Johnny that they should leave the area. She told him that Ronnie's body was definitely there and that Nancy should be taken away. She said she would feign illness, so as not to arouse Nancy's suspicions.

"Are you sure it's Ronnie you're feeling?" the boy asked.

"Of course I'm sure," Dorothy said.

"Well, they did find a black boy's body here about a month ago. Maybe you're sensing him," Johnny offered.

"Not on your life," Dorothy exclaimed. She moved toward Nancy.

Nancy was confused and angry when Dorothy said she wanted to leave. After so much enthusiasm and confidence, Nancy had expected to spend the whole day out looking.

But Nancy could not dissuade the psychic. She was aware that she wasn't paying Dorothy anything, so Dorothy was free to do as she pleased. Nancy placed the vase on the ground and the two women walked slowly back to the car.

Before Dorothy drove to Nutley, she told Nancy that someone in a blue car would have important information for her. "Whatever he says is crucial," she told the sad mother.

Dorothy told the police by telephone that they should search the fields around Teterboro. If someone had been buried there in September, the changes of season would have washed away any indications. The police said they didn't have the manpower to search such a large area.

Chapter 8

March was a strong month for Dorothy, a period in which her success rate always soared high. For reasons best explained astrologically, Dorothy's life seemed to take its most dramatic turns during March.

Ten years before, Dorothy had only been able to handle one case at a time; now she was working on as many as twenty at once. Many of the early frustrations had been shed over the years as she learned to believe in herself. She still had to deal with chance at every turn, never knowing if her vision would ever connect with reality. So many times she wished she had been able to resolve cases such as the Delardo-Carlucci murders, but she had long ago learned to take things as they were. Still, she would never give up hoping that one day she would find the murderers in unresolved cases.

Requests for Dorothy's help and guidance now numbered well over a thousand. From early morning to late at night her two phones rang with pleas from all over the United States and with latest information on cases. Both police and parents made a haven of her home.

Dorothy had strong feelings about Ronnie Stica; she was certain that Nancy would have her son back, albeit a corpse, within days. She told Nancy about the Jacobsons and how they had suffered for the past twenty-two months, not certain if their daughter was alive or dead.

Nancy phoned Dorothy on Easter Sunday wondering if Dorothy had any feelings about an article Nancy had seen in a newspaper. The skeleton of a boy had been found in an oil drum at the bottom of a twelve-foot shaft in Staten Island. He was decomposed, Nancy said, except for a pair of sneakers. Ronnie had worn tennis shoes, and the body had apparently been there a long time. Did Dorothy have any feelings about it?

"It's not Ronnie, Nancy. I feel certain it isn't Ronnie. Your boy is not on Staten Island, he's closer to home. But maybe it's Susan Jacobson."

"Can't be," Nancy said. "The article says it's a boy."

"That doesn't matter," Dorothy informed her. "Sometimes it takes days of lab work to figure out whether a skeleton is male or female. Something tells me the shaft you're reading about is one I've seen."

Bill Jacobson had been reading the evening newspaper at his office in Wall Street, when he noticed a piece about three kids muscrat-hunting in Mariner's Harbor, and finding the decomposed body of a youngster. He phoned Ellen, who in turn called the police to see if the body was Susan's.

After several conversations and no answers, she figured out for herself that the corpse had to be Susan. One of the detectives reported that the tennis shoes found bore some writing, although all that was legible was "4-ever" and two blurred names. At one time, Ellen knew, those two names had been "Susan-Dempsey."

Ellen called Dorothy to tell her that Susan had been found. The body had been spotted by a thirteen-year-old boy who was playing with friends in the area. He had seen the skeleton sticking out of a fifty-five-gallon oil drum at the bottom of a twelve-foot concrete shaft.

The fact that would wrench the heart of Bill Jacobson ever afterward was that he had been in the very shaft where Susan was found when Dorothy had pointed it out to him. It had then been partially full of water, and the oil drum, which Dorothy had smelled so acutely, prevented anyone from seeing or smelling the decomposing body.

It was also the very place to which Dempsey had taken Patricia Jacobson in search of her sister. Dempsey, never descending into the shaft, only pointed out places he felt the others might look.

News of the discovery and Dorothy's involvement spread quickly through New York's media. On Monday the *New York Post* ran a major story with Susan's picture on the front page. The following day the *Post* ran a large story about Dorothy with the headline, "Psychic Sees a New Job: Finding S.I. Girl's Killer."

Everyone's eyes turned to Illinois where Dempsey Hawkins was living with his father and grandmother. Within days, the process of extradition began, to bring the boy back for arraignment.

Dorothy was even more excited when, the next Tuesday, Nancy Locascio phoned to report that Ronnie's body had been found in the area behind Teterboro Airport.

She told Dorothy that one of Joey's friends had come to their house on the weekend. When Nancy opened the door, she saw the anxious boy was driving a blue car. Remembering Dorothy's words about the car, Nancy felt instinctively the teen-ager was there for more than just a friendly visit.

He said he wanted to talk with Joey. The two boys left the house immediately, and Nancy waited anxiously for her son to return. Joey came home two hours later saying that the friend had told him the three boys responsible for killing Ronnie had heard that the police had been led by the psychic to the Teterboro Airport area, and that the search was centered there. The friend reported that Ronnie was, indeed, there, and had been killed by Dave Menicola with a knife. The wound that had taken Menicola to the hospital was a knife wound, not a glass cut. What grieved Nancy most was the fact that three boys had been involved in the murder, and that Ronnie's murder was well known to the teen-agers who frequented the wall.

At Susan's funeral, Bill Jacobson realized that the "John and Mary tombstone" of Dorothy's last hypnosis session had at last been found. The "silver" she had seen was "Silva Funeral Parlor." Susan's burial was at St. Peter's cemetery, the grave located not two hundred feet behind what had once been stables owned by John and Mary Moore. The tract of ground now used for burial had once been a bridle path. Dorothy had seen horses from the past taking her to a burying place in the future.

Bail for Dempsey was set initially at $100,000, but at the request of Hawkins's attorney, the judge ordered the eighteen-year-old youth held without bail until a formal application for bail could be made. But the prosecution already had a strong case against Dempsey. The district attorney's office said it intended to produce witnesses—not necessarily eyewitnesses—who had identified Dempsey as the murderer. Dempsey entered a plea of innocent.

Susan had been with Dempsey at his apartment that Saturday afternoon. They had quarreled about breaking up the relationship and had walked along the railroad tracks toward Mariner's Harbor. After Dempsey strangled Susan to death and hid her body in the oil drum, he had gone home and changed shirts and then gone directly to the nearby playground where he informed his cousin Punky of his deed. Later he had taken his cousin to Mariner's Harbor and pointed out the shaft. Not only Punky but several other teen-agers knew of the murder, but no one had said a thing. At Dempsey's trial Punky was the chief witness against him.

Mrs. Hawkins refused to discuss the case when questioned by reporters. "Please don't ask me any questions," she said.

Dempsey's sentencing was held on April 6, 1979. That week Dorothy had been in Johnstown, New York, working on a case concerning a teen-ager who had been abducted from a local bar. She returned early on that Friday to attend the sentencing with the Jacobsons. She had not attended any of the long trial, careful, as always, not to jeopardize the prosecution's case with publicity about psychics. But Dorothy had spent twenty-two months with the Jacobsons and had held out for Dempsey's reckoning.

In the courtroom Mrs. Hawkins sat alone and erect during the proceedings, across the aisle from Dorothy and the Jacobsons. When Dempsey was brought into the courtroom, his head was held high and his expression was impassive, even while his attorney pleaded with the judge to impose the minimum prison term of fifteen years.

The middle-aged lawyer stood before the judge and stated that the murder had not been premeditated or carried out for financial gain. He said it had been the "emotional explosion" of a teen-ager confused by love and society. He argued that Dempsey could not have been "totally bad" if the Jacobson family had "condoned and accepted him" until the time of the abortion. He claimed that Dempsey had been raised in an unjust society, one in which his place had never been comfortable.

Dempsey Hawkins was sentenced to a mandatory life term. He would serve a minimum prison term of twenty-two years before parole consideration. The maximum the judge could have set was twenty-five years.

Dempsey's mother quietly sobbed into her hands as her son passed by. Dorothy felt sorry for her, but as for the son, she felt justice had been served.

For the Jacobsons the long ordeal—and all the unanswered questions—were finally over. What remained for Ellen and Bill Jacobson was the heartbreak of having lost a beautiful daughter in the springtime of her life. The memory of that loss would always haunt them, but Dorothy knew that for the Jacobsons life was still worth living: they were blessed with six other children, and their home abounded with love. And out of the terrible sorrow of the Jacobson case, a deep, abiding relationship had grown between Dorothy and the Jacobsons. Ellen and Bill considered her a member of their family.

The long, arduous trial of Ronnie Stica's murderer extended even longer the agony that his mother had suffered. Looking around the courtroom, she saw other teen-agers who might have known, since September, that her son had been murdered, but who had chosen to say nothing.

Preliminary medical examinations had revealed that Ronnie had been stabbed once in the throat and three times in the upper back. Three boys had downed her son. During the trial it was brought out that the Teterboro site had not been a totally arbitrary choice. Several feet from Ronnie's body was a patch of cultivating cannabis plants, which one of the group had harvested without anyone else knowing about it. Menicola suspected Ronnie.

The two friends who accompanied Menicola to the murder site claimed to have no idea that a murder was about to transpire. They were given two and three years with probations. Dave Menicola, twenty years old, was given twenty-six years, without parole.

The discovery site of Ronnie's body couldn't have been closer to Dorothy's description. Nancy could not bear to think he had been murdered not more than ten feet away from the white ceramic vase she had held. She cried, knowing how close to her own son she had been without being able to feel his presence. When Dorothy went to the site herself, she looked around the area and saw, across the highway, a billboard with the word "Eclipse" standing out. Ronnie's body was hidden directly behind the Eclipse Bowling Alley.

Dorothy's life was now totally consumed by her work. She had helped resolve over thirty cases, and aided and searched in more than a hundred. As her successes increased and her name spread across the country, more and more requests for her help appeared. In the next year the number of letters handled by Lupo and Phyllis would reach as high as nine thousand.

The resolution of the Jacobson and Stica cases within days of one another triggered even greater publicity for Dorothy, who suddenly had not only mothers chasing her for help, but news reporters from *Newsweek*, *McCall's*, and *Readers Digest*, approaching her as well. Calls came from television talk shows across America, requesting Dorothy as a guest.

She was proud of her work and the respect she was suddenly accorded. She would gladly go on television with her own special message: a child is never safe enough. Dorothy would campaign against lazy, negligent parenthood. Words of caution directed at children and teen-agers would be: avoid dealing with total strangers; open up communication within families. She wanted parents to understand how different their children's lives might be from their own childhoods.

In her fifties Dorothy was younger and more energetic than ever. Her family was proud of her success and so were the many detectives and police who had watched her evolve into a famous sleuth. Her big moment would come that summer when she addressed the International Association for Identification in Baltimore, speaking before federal investigators and agents from all over the Northeast.

Suddenly she understood what the fortune-teller and her own mother had said: she would stand alone. Her uniqueness gave her life a richness she had never imagined possible. When she thought of her mother and her present life, she felt positive that Appolonia had known all that was to happen to the little girl from Jersey City.